Literacy

in a

Multimedia Age

Literacy

in a

Multimedia Age

Dennis Adams
Mary Hamm

Christopher-Gordon Publishers, Inc.
Norwood, Massachusetts

Credits

Every effort has been made to contact copyright holders for permission to reproduce borrowed material where necessary. We apologize for any oversights and would be happy to rectify them in future prints.

Christopher-Gordon Publishers, Inc.
1502 Providence Highway, Suite 12
Norwood, MA 02062
1-800-934-8322
781-762-5577

Printed in the United States of America

10 9 8 7 6 5 4 3 2 1   06 05 04 03 02 01

Library of Congress Catalog Card Number: 2001088606

ISBN: 1-929024-31-2

Contents

vii | Introduction

1 | **Chapter 1**
Literacy, Learning, and New Media: How Technology is Reshaping the Way Education is Practiced

33 | **Chapter 2**
Media Production: Storyboards, Video, Computers, and More

55 | **Chapter 3**
Collaborative Inquiry: Working Together to Accomplish Shared Goals

89 | **Chapter 4**
Process Skills Across the Curriculum: Interdisciplinary Themes, Engaging Student Understandings

123 | **Chapter 5**
Technological Literacy: Teaching, Learning, Culture, and Technology

145 | **Chapter 6**
The Internet: Changing the Way We Teach and Learn

187 | Glossary

197 | Index

199 | The Authors

Introduction

Literacy used to be confined to the space between reading and writing. In traditional school-based settings, students often spent more time learning isolated reading skills than learning the types of literacy they were most likely to use in life. By the 1990s there was general agreement that when students engage in one aspect of literacy, other communication skills came into play. Literacy came to be viewed as the ability to communicate in real-world situations, which involves the ability to read, write, speak, listen, think, and view. Viewing is particularly important to the emerging view of literacy. It is the process of looking critically at visual information in a television production, a movie, a video game, an Internet Web site, or a computer simulation. In the 21st century literacy will involve going beyond interpretation to the creation of meaning with converging information and communication technology.

Literacy in a Multimedia Age extends the literacy umbrella to include media analysis, multimedia production, collaborative inquiry, networking technologies, and more. We view media as a junction point between disciplines that can serve as a vehicle for pulling fragmented elements of the curriculum together. Because literacy in one subject influences literacy in another, we provide thematic linking activities. Current literacy issues, media trends, and practical teaching activities are viewed as building blocks for the technology-intensive multiliteracies needed in the 21st century. The new world of cyberspace is bound to transform the nature of literacy and learning. Our goal is to help teachers and their students understand, use, and create with the most powerful media available.

The meaning of literacy changes as new circumstances, new technologies, and new approaches to teaching open a wider range of possibilities. For many the word *literacy* has become almost synonymous with the word *competence*. Although we do not push the definition that far, a multitude of technologically intensive literacies are considered: media literacy, computer literacy, information literacy, visual literacy, technology literacy, and networking literacy.

New media technologies have significant educational, cultural, political, and economic implications for the new century. This book views the rapidly expanding digital environment and encourages readers to think intelligently about its effect on their lives. It also gives teachers practical suggestions for using technological tools in a way that supports their efforts to do a better job in new ways. Television has been the big kid on the electronic block for 50 years. The most visible of the newer technologies that teachers need to contend with are the computer and the Internet. They provide us with the opportunity and the power to shape the new rules by which we want to live. With this power comes a greater ability to be heard across the world, to find information, and to exercise or abuse our rights. Along with all of this comes a greater responsibility for our actions and the world that we are creating.

What will it mean to be literate in the 21st century? *Literacy in a Multimedia Age* attempts to answer that question. It is written in a style that, we hope, teachers and prospective teachers will find accessible. Many easy-to-do media-related activities have been included. These methods are based on the belief that children build knowledge about media from their own experiences. The suggestion here is that knowledge cannot be gained simply by absorption through the senses. Whatever the subject, active thinking and collaborative doing are essential characteristics of effective instruction. This constructivist approach to teaching is consistent with brain-based learning.

Children need access to the most powerful media available so that they can examine reality from many angles and in different lights. As they use media to engage in social, physical, and mental activities, it is possible to visualize new connections and choices. These concepts are compatible with cognitive research and Howard Gardner's multiple intelligence theories. The use of the full range of digital tools can help to open multiple pathways to a subject. Whiz-bang high-tech skills are useful, but sound fundamentals like individual judgment, social values, and teamwork are key to handling today's technology. Knowledgeable teachers have shown that it is possible to be educated, thoughtful, confident, and fully aware of the technological possibilities.

Literacy, Learning, and New Media:
How Technology Is Reshaping the Way Education Is Practiced

Technology is only one of the many forces driving human history, and seldom the most important. Technology only gives us tools. Human desires and institutions decide how we use them.
—Freeman J. Dyson

Technology is changing the nature of literacy, learning, and more. Literacy now requires an understanding of information and communication technology. It also requires manipulating the processes used to create messages in the modern world. Wise teachers realize that they cannot avoid today's technological realities if they are going to prepare students for life in a new knowledge-based society. They also realize that certain kinds of technical knowledge becomes outdated so fast that we really have to train people beyond technical expertise.

We now see more and more references to technological literacy, visual literacy, networking literacy, and information literacy. Librarians define *information literacy* as the ability to know when information is needed; as well as the ability to identify, locate, and effectively use information for problem solving and lifelong learning (Association for Educational Communications and Technologies and the American Association of School Librarians, 1998). More literacies are lurking out there on the technological horizon. As a result, today's students must learn how to decode, understand, and create messages with many forms of print and nonprint media. Reading and writing will remain central instructional concerns, but it is also clear that anyone who wants to successfully navigate his or her way through the 21st century has to grasp the nature of the more fluid and dynamic interconnectedness that is made possible by newer technology.

As educators learn to explore new and more effective ways to do their jobs in a new era, they are constantly trying to figure out how they can make the best of human and machine possibilities. Both literally and metaphorically, educators can be sure that the walls of the school will become more permeable. Technology will certainly alter the way we organize knowledge and, as a result, ourselves. In the 21st century, a parade of new multimedia devices and networked software is bound to change how we teach and learn in significant ways.

Although electronic media can complement the social nature of learning, it cannot take the place of face-to-face social interaction. The idea of collaborative inquiry in small heterogeneous groups has long appealed to teachers on several levels. One reason that teachers like to put three or four students together for cooperative groups is that it helps the teachers to deal with increasingly diverse classrooms in a way that accommodates individual differences in achievement. The more isolated learners are physically or socially, the more they need access to peers, learning communities, and other social resources. Technology can help by providing access to multiple communities, directly and indirectly, purposely and serendipitously (Brown & Duguid, 2000). The various standards projects have also pointed out that communication and information technologies can play an important social role as integrating and collaborative forces in the classroom.

Digital Technologies, Social Interaction, and Intellectual Development

Everything from books to the movies seems to have a digital future in sight. Elements of different technologies are increasingly overlapping with each other and with basic subject matter. As new interlocking media increasingly shape our future, it is important to tap the possibilities and solve some of the pedagogical problems.

There are certainly many contradictory phenomena that coexist as we try to come to terms with a multimedia age and its educational, social, and economic fallout. The power of today's information, communication, and networking technologies requires special and sustained attention. With any new medium, serious pedagogical thought and preparation must precede a warm educational welcome. Will developing multimedia technology provide a transforming vision and a new awareness? Probably so, but there are many possible futures out there for new media and associated digital technologies.

Multiple technology-intensive literacies increasingly cut across subject matter at school and day-to-day life in general. The habits of mind fostered through such visually intensive media interactions need to be understood by everybody. Take "media literacy" as an example. It moves beyond teaching through media to teaching about and creating with media. Comprehending, analyzing, composing, and appreciating multiple print and nonprint symbol systems are all part of today's literacy equation. So are parents, media makers, and others who shape the hearts and minds of children and young adults.

Whiz-bang technology cannot replace concrete experiences. Children learn best when they can do things in three dimensions. Direct human interaction is much better for them than a constant barrage of frenzied images on a two-dimensional screen. Whether it's the television, the computer, or the Web, a little developmentally appropriate programming won't hurt school-age children, in our view. Nevertheless, electronic media is most enjoyable and informative when a friend or an adult shares the experience. It's best for teachers to shape the role of technology now, because in the future we will all be interacting with a wider range of media possibilities. In tomorrow's schools, electronic media will be experienced as "texts" to be appreciated, analyzed, created, and shared.

Navigating Electronic Highways

"On the Internet, nobody knows you're a dog." In the last 10 years you could count on seeing this 1993 cartoon caption cited, without reference to *The New Yorker*, in articles on Internet privacy and anonymity. It has even been put into programming code (Java), copied onto T-shirts, used as a title for a play, and prominently displayed on thousands of Web sites. On the Internet, it seems, nobody knows who coins a popular phrase before it becomes an old saying and slips into a shared public memory bank. As Peter Steiner, the original designer of the smiley face, has pointed out, it's a little like citing who first sketched the smiley face. Now that "old phrase" or "adage" is about to be overtaken by technology. Thanks to Webcams and Netcams, Internet anonymity is fading. Skidder beware, soon everyone will know that you're a dog.

Active, hands-on electronic learning is now available for students with networked computers all over the world. Internet technology puts all kinds of worldwide possibilities at the student's fingertips. Learning how to sort valid information from a glut of misinformation is becoming more important than ever. The following questions have to be asked:

- Who created this?
- Is the source commercial, public gossip, or solid research?
- What are the credentials of the writer or producer?
- How accurate and up-to-date is the information?

Now, more than ever, we have to learn how to sort out the real and the reliable from the unreal and the questionable. Students need to know what's worth knowing, and they need to acquire the discipline to focus on academics in the face of glittering distractions. Having an intellectual and moral compass for sorting through the glut of information certainly helps, as does the acquisition of the intellectual tools for constructing meaning, interpreting information, and assessing information.

As it becomes increasingly difficult to separate reality from virtual reality, the only constant is the roller-coaster ride of change itself. It is little wonder that a student's day-to-day world often feels out of joint. To function in today's media-saturated environment, students need to be informed by a solid knowledge base. Creating meaning and communicating effectively with a multitude of media is now a key literacy ingredient. Educated citizens must be able to evaluate their media choices, understand the underlying values, and use available media tools for expression. No matter how stunning or entrancing, new media will not negate the wisdom of the ages or allow us to escape our limitations, because every medium is, in many respects, an extension of ourselves.

When a new medium comes along, it often changes the shape of ideas, how we think, and the nature of human communication. The dimensions of change usually aren't clear until much later. The possibilities of the print media, for example, didn't become clear until well after it was on the scene. After Johannes Gutenberg turned his wine press into a printing press, it took more than 50 years before someone thought of numbering the pages. Of course, 50 years of technological change in the 15th century may translate into 50 months in the 21st century. One constant is that it is still a race between new media and wise human applications.

If a technology is not well understood, there is a tendency to either overstate its possibilities or dismiss its promise. Exaggerations can kill an instructional tool before it has a chance to develop. Only rarely does anyone accurately predict the full impact of new technologies. No matter how flashy, if a medium debases the culture, panders to violent impulses, isolates us from one another, or diminishes the impact of a caring community, we have to change it or get rid of it. Will it lead to utopia or disaster?

The truth is usually somewhere in between. Some things are bound to be missed, but everything possible must be done to make sure that information and communications technology will be used to spark a renaissance in human learning, thinking, and communication.

The *aeolipile* ("wind ball") designed by Heron was a forerunner of both the steam engine and the jet engine.

Figure 1-1. An earlier form of technological development: Heron's "windball"

Long-Term, Carefully Planned Commitments

Schools have received so much conflicting and changing advice on technological issues that it is little wonder that teachers seem reticent. Applications relevant to a constantly changing workplace take more and more time away from other subjects. The problem is that the more mechanical aspects of technology and programming become outdated so fast that students have to be educated beyond a narrow band of workplace skills. Teamwork, critical thinking, citizenship, and intellectual curiosity all override specific vocational skills in importance.

Today we have the Internet and e-mail, and we encourage students to create their own World Wide Web pages. Many of these things make sense, but they also overwhelm teachers. Whenever we set out to change the schools, simple short-term solutions often turn out to be illusions. The reexamination that is part of implementing new technologies can assist change, but like any other innovation, its successful use will take sustained and carefully planned commitments.

In the last two decades, teachers have often found themselves caught between shifting advice and paltry support for professional development. No matter how conscientious they are, they end up getting blamed for foot-dragging by techno-enthusiasts in industry and government. The human, physical, and pedagogical infrastructure necessary for full-scale integration of technology into the teaching and learning process is simply not in place in many American schools. Many things have to happen before schools can more fully integrate modern technology into the curriculum. To begin with, we have to improve the working conditions in the schools, pay for professional development time, and give teachers more control over the process. At the same time, those designing the technology have to build reliability and educational possibilities into their products.

The newer the media, the less we know about it. Fortunately, some of the findings from print and television apply to digital technologies. No matter what we do, technology is bound to have an ever more powerful effect on cognitive development, learning, and literacy. We might as well try to bend it in a favorable direction. Every age seeks out the appropriate medium to confront the question of human existence. Ours just happens to be electronic and increasingly digital.

We can be sure that the increased power of multimedia technologies will result in many more changes in teaching and learning patterns. Sophisticated visual models can trigger much more profound thinking. Greater care needs to be taken, however, in what is presented to children, for they often rely on visual learning rather than conceptual knowledge. The video screen has been a potent tool in presenting visual experiences to viewers that they inevitably accept. In spite of the power of the visual image, however, verbal explanations, personal experience, and active learning in the classroom are bound to have a continuing impact on the learning experience.

Before schools put more resources into buying computers or wiring classrooms for the Internet, we need to identify significant instructional problems that the technology is going to help us solve. The next step is to concentrate on the pedagogical plan and to be sure to pay attention to access and equity. Teachers' needs and professional development should be a top priority all along the way.

New Media Symbology Shapes the Communication Process

Each communication medium makes use of its own distinctive technology for gathering, encoding, sorting, and conveying its contents associated with different situations. The technological nature of a medium affects the interaction with its users, just as the method for transmitting content affects the knowledge acquired. However, far from becoming less important, human sociability becomes even more important in an era of bits and bytes.

We live in a complex society dependent on rapid communication and information access. Television, film, computers, and the Internet are rapidly becoming our dominant cultural tools for selecting, gathering, storing, and conveying knowledge in representational forms. Not only that—children are spending nearly 30 hours a week at home and more than 7 hours a week at school interacting with television sets and computers. It is little wonder that the various standards projects point to the importance of students developing the skills necessary for interpreting and processing all kinds of media messages. We can reasonably expect the texture of learning to change.

A system of symbols governs what is presented either in print or in some kind of visual representation. Specific mental skills need to be learned in order to gather, decode, and assimilate internal representations germane to each symbolic system. In learning how to read, for instance, children need to figure out sound-symbol relationships between the letters. To understand what they're reading, they need an experiential context and an appropriate vocabulary they can use to articulate their interpretations. Similar skills are required when making sense out of visual imagery. However, dealing with a constant barrage of electronic images, either on the television set or on the computer monitor as one surfs the Net to extract meaningful content, is no small task. Unfortunately, higher level discriminative powers do not just happen. Careful instruction precedes an intelligent weeding out of useless data and the interpretation and processing of potentially informative visual imagery.

Although different media forms share some characteristics, they do have their own distinguishing features in the way they convey meaning. Print relies heavily on the reader's ability to interpret abstract symbols. The video screen appears to demand less of the viewer, because content is communicated more directly through visual imagery. The Internet is a hybrid of both modes of learning.

It turns out that children are influenced more by content than by the delivery system itself, so no matter what medium is used, quality of programming is key. Educational designers must also take advantage of unique media attributes and the specific mental skills they address in order to accommodate various learning styles. Research studies show that children learn much more effectively when the way information is physically presented matches the way it is mentally represented. Whatever route is taken, the consistent formula almost always appears to be that better communication equals easier processing and more transfer. Fortunately, electronic media can facilitate both voluntary attention and the formation of ideas and concepts in children.

New educational choices are being laid open by information and communication technologies (Figure 1-2). Understanding and employing these technological forces require a critical perspective that interprets new literacies from a unique perspective.

Using Technology's Powers to Motivate Learners

While the technological infrastructure is being laid for an information-intensive educational environment, commensurate attention should be given to articulating an appropriate philosophy of teaching and learning cognizant of new high-tech realities. Unleashing unlimited global sources of knowledge for the human mind to tap into lifts the learning experience several levels up, not unlike the major shift that occurred when society moved from an oral to a written culture. What we need is an intellectual framework that will articulate new learning possibilities that should be made available to all. This is where technology might have a place. However, to ensure that the tone and priorities of learning in a democratic society serve the best interests of all, this nation must balance its moral, intellectual, financial, and technological capital.

Computer-based tools have been developed to enhance higher level human mental processing. For instance, the Internet has used hypermedia technology to allow users to click on what are called "hyperlinks." These are usually blue, underlined phrases that connect to other Web documents that will further explain the concepts in which the user is interested. These documents,

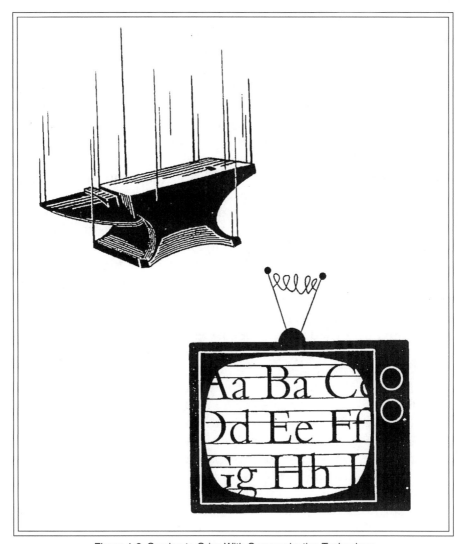

Figure 1-2. Coming to Grips With Communication Technology

in turn, are stored in different Web servers scattered throughout the world. Hyperlinks allow us to pursue our trend of thought wherever it may take us. This is great for things like creative brainstorming. This is one case where technology assists rather than hinders intellectual adventures and unpredictable meanderings.

Users of a PC machine may also open one or several windows simultaneously, using Web browsers such as Netscape Navigator or Internet Explorer, multitask, and selectively hop down a number of database alleys. The Internet is then like a library with all of the books dumped in piles on the floor. Search en-

gines like "Google," "Ask Jeeves," or "Metacrawler"—no matter
how well engineered they are—are still blunt devices that are not
all that good at cutting through the information glut. A step up
from the search engines are "bots," which roam the vast expanses
of cyberspace in search of the specific information that we need.
New services have been offered lately using "personal guides" or
"subject matter experts" to make the online information search a
much more humanized, less frustrating, and, hopefully, more
productive task.

Integrated information systems, Web appliances, and wireless devices are already on the scene. Television will not be left
too far behind. WebTV has been around for some time. Soon we
will have artificially intelligent high-definition television sets that
will present movie quality sight and sound as it learns what is of
most interest to the viewer. These systems are beginning to be
capable of combing extensive databases and networks to assemble
programs that are specifically tailored for the viewer. Personal
computers and their digital associates are transforming themselves into networked video processing machines. As images from
every direction begin to flood through our consciousness, there
is still much more to come.

Working with new multimedia tools will still require keeping
up with the "basics." Teachers will still need a thorough knowledge of subject matter as well as an understanding of multimedia tools. Furthermore, principles of effective instruction should
guide how the two areas can work together. Collaboratively writing a one- or two-page philosophy of teaching statement is a
good way for teachers to engage in purposeful inquiry into their
ideas about teaching and learning. Practice can then be guided
by what they discover. In addition, such reflection and discussion with a colleague can provide a sound foundation for professional and personal growth throughout the year.

As educators reach for a mobilizing vision, there's no need to
settle for obvious solutions or to accept recent social, educational, or technological limitations. Sometimes it's better to look
around than to look ahead. Cyberspace, for example, has become more like a television home shopping channel than the
fabulous educational medium that was advertised in the mid-
1990s.

Having been around for more than half a century, television
has many lessons to teach us. One of those lessons is that there
are many paths to a mistake. On TV, the interests of the advertisers usually come before those of the viewer. Advertisements
sanctify, signify, mythologize, and fantasize economic and political structures. Along the way they help to shape American cul-

ture. Becoming an intelligent consumer of media now requires learning to critically analyze the structure and methods of advertising. Similarly, in using an Internet search engine, the ads start jumping up all over the place.

The telephone, radio, and television are examples of old media that are less glamorous than the multimedia Web. However, they work as they are supposed to almost every time. No one would put up with waiting 10 or 20 seconds to change a station, or accept a telephone system where he couldn't get a dial tone once or twice a day. The Internet has a long way to go because of the time, experience, and technological breakthroughs that are needed to operate much more complicated technical systems. PC software, access networks, and core networks all have to build in greater reliability and faster data streams if the Web is going to be the mass medium of the 21st century.

Our expanding knowledge of how children learn can inform our work as we set out to build technology into the schools of tomorrow. There is general agreement that technology is an important thing, but it's not the only thing. As far as the schools are concerned, the human side of education is critical. The task ahead is to build on every human and technological possibility to make quality education more broadly accessible.

Changing Patterns of Human Communication

The doctrine of "overconnectedness" is spreading across the industrialized world like wildfire. An unintended consequence of the Internet era is the shrinkage of the distance between work and play. Telecommunications have evolved to the point where citizens can get on line with cell phones, palm pilots, laptop computers, and an odd assortment of wireless devices. Now everyone can connect to everyone else all the time, anywhere. It may be great for business, but it leaves little private breathing space in our lives. Changes that appear to be trivial in the beginning can end up causing a fundamental shift in human ways of knowing and perceiving.

Understanding how evolving electronic systems affect educational, cultural, perceptual, and social organization means learning how to ask the right conceptual questions. Helping children to become critical consumers of electronically produced information is a major societal responsibility. With all too little thought, imagery-intensive technology is releasing conceptualizing power that is as hard to control as a raging river. For example, the fast pace of electronic media often leaves little room for personal or social reflection.

What's the difference between technology and a medium? Technology might be thought of as a hardwired creation. A medium is more of a social construct. The same technology can be used in a multitude of ways, depending on the cultural context. The technology of television, for example, can be used as visual wallpaper, a moneymaking machine, propaganda, trash, or a tool to illuminate learning.

The full range of electronic media, however, can be anything between an intellectually rich adventure and a manipulative bore. It can rob us of time or empower us with knowledge. Whether it enhances or diminishes life depends on how we shape it.

Cultivating "Information Age" Mindsets for Electronic Literacy

Information conveyed by television is frequently removed from any realistic social context. In this atmosphere, journalism, politics, and religion are turned into forms of entertainment. Add music, film, and the Internet and you will see American popular culture altering information, communication, and entertainment in cultures around the world.

Increasing numbers of electronic devices, video applications, and courseware are not neutral. They represent essential characteristics that are already changing the nature of work, recreation, and learning. The dominant visual format of commercial American media has little tolerance for intelligent argument, guesswork, questioning, or explanation. Substance and logic are often replaced by image, gesture, and the values of merchandising and show business. The very nature of the medium often leaves little to the imagination or intellect—sound cues even tell us which emotion or mood is appropriate.

In one guise or another, the video screen is becoming a major informational and educational delivery system. Today electronically produced visual imagery is being called upon to play a more fundamental role in thinking, learning, and experiencing products of the mind. The longtime collision among art, commerce, and the public good continues at an intensified pace.

Children's view of fact, fiction, and traditional literacy is largely influenced by the visual imagery to which they are exposed. Entertainment is often viewed as representing social reality, in spite of an accumulation of life experiences that suggest the opposite. Children, for example, are able to recognize books as fiction long before they are able to recognize what's real or unreal on TV or on the Internet (Adams, 2000).

There are a number of trends that are cause for serious concern. We are now a culture in which ideas, information, and ways of knowing are more shaped by the video screen than by newspapers, books, or magazines. One unfortunate result of this trend is that nearly a quarter of American adults have trouble comprehending a well-written paragraph. The literacy umbrella may cover a broader range of media, but not being able to read and write still condemns a person to the bottom of the economic barrel.

The main goal of any medium is involvement. No matter what the nature of the medium, its own technological base should allow for various forms of synthetic form-making activity in the user's mind. Print or video imagery, for instance, could involve the user's attention to matters of fact, perceiving analogies, drawing inferences, and personally delineating distinctions. To help people reach a higher level of media exploration, the major goal should be to make any medium interesting, involving, and life enhancing.

Literacy Activities That Connect Home and School

> Communicating is a process of sharing experience till it becomes a common possession. It modifies the disposition of both parties who partake it.
>
> —John Dewey

Children learn about reading and writing in active ways. They can construct their own meaning using various language tools to communicate. This means interacting with peers, using meaningful stories to accomplish genuine purposes. The goal of adult mediation should be to provide information that students need to know when they need to know it. It is up to teachers and parents to create a literate environment and mediate the learning that occurs by modeling the use of literacy activities.

Whatever adults want to make important to children, they must make important to themselves as well. For example, it's hard for teachers to teach reading if they don't (at least occasionally) read books themselves. Likewise, it's hard for a parent to instill a love of literature if there are no reading materials (books, magazines, and newspapers) around the house. Reading the environment precedes reading the world.

Parents today are more of a diverse group than ever. Some parents can't read themselves. Those who can are most likely to be working outside the home. Therefore, helping with an in-home connection to literacy is more complex than ever. Parents need to know what's going on in school so that they can help out at home. When teachers change their methods and classroom organizational structures, they need the understanding of parents, administrators, and other teachers. Some teachers meet with parents before school starts to set cooperative goals and ask parents about the child's strong and weak points—what works for the child and what doesn't. Parents can make a big contribution to their child's success in school by helping children to use reading, writing, listening, and speaking for real purposes.

Some of the practices that encourage literacy at home are similar to those that work in the classroom. Language learning, at its best, is a shared experience. At home this means stories at bedtime, a discussion of the news, adults who read, museum excursions, and library visits. Reading, writing, and creative language experiences help to develop the capacity for an aesthetic response to literature. At school it's up to the teacher to make sure that literacy instruction builds on the outside experiences with the strategies necessary for meaningful reading and writing.

Programs with literature-based components have a foundation built on collaboration and a belief that literacy instruction should be natural, holistic, and connected to a strong literary base. This powerful approach to literacy development requires intrinsically motivating activities that help students to draw on their cultural and personal resources as they develop productive habits of the mind. Engaging youngsters in an active group exploration of ideas is exciting.

For the seeds of literacy to grow, teachers must take themselves seriously as agents of change who arrange classroom environments for cooperation, problem solving, and engagement. Providing a rich, engaging, literary environment for all children means recognizing that children have different pathways to literacy. Taking *some* path is essential. Literacy gives students new tools for reflecting on a whole range of communication possibilities. It also gives them new capacities for personal and social action.

The methods chosen to teach language skills will probably reflect a unique combination of professional knowledge, policy requirements, student background, and personal choice. The degree of success for an integrated language arts approach to learning depends upon the background and enthusiasm of the teacher. To paraphrase William Blake, energy is an external delight. If teachers are energized and really believe in literature-based language instruction, they usually do just fine—even if they have to wait for the system to catch up.

E-Books: A New Wave in Reading and Language Arts

A few years ago you could find only a small number of electronic books stored at universities. A few were available over the Internet, but most were completely unavailable. Until 2000 they were hard to access, and it was even harder to read the scrolling text. Today there are tens of thousands of titles that are available in different formats on several devices. They have become easy to get and much easier to read. Major publishers have jumped on the bandwagon and are now selling a range of titles designed to be read on hand-held computers called Readers.

Microsoft Reader, Softbook, Rocket eBook, NuvoMedia, and their associates are complicating the publishing business, to say nothing of reading and language arts instruction. Hardware companies like Compaq, Casio, and Hewlett-Packard are rolling out palm- to book-sized reading devices. Colorful and cute, they come loaded with ClearType from Microsoft or CoolType from Adobe. This software smoothes the jagged edges of electronic type in a way that makes the words on the screen much easier to read.

Electronic book devices cost several hundred dollars and can hold the equivalent of 5 to 10 books at a time. Titles can be delivered over the Internet in a few minutes. Some of the Readers, like Softbook, can simply be plugged into a telephone line for downloading. Whatever the platform, nonfiction works can be constantly upgraded and books can be customized so that the user can read only certain parts. Special features also allow the user to adjust the size of the print, the sound, or the background lighting. Unlike paper books, e-books can be read in the dark.

E-book Readers are able to search for strings of ideas or words within the text and quickly find information, interesting passages, and references. A menu lets readers jump quickly to a particular chapter or a favorite scene. E-book software can even read out loud in ways that reinforce the speaking and listening dimensions of language and literacy. Children are very attracted to these digital reading tools. A common question when they see one is, "When can I read my books on one of these?"

Microsoft and some of their associates believe that a sea change from paper to electronic books is on the horizon, but don't count on it. Paper books will *not* "go the way of the quill pen." E-books are, however, finding a comfortable niche in the publishing world, along with Web appliances, broadband Web access, Palm Pilots, and other wireless communication technologies. Digital technologies will increasingly reshape the way education is practiced. Although much of language arts instruction will continue along traditional paths, the schools cannot avoid the most powerful information and communication technologies of our time.

In spite of inevitable changes, the wood-pulp business has little to fear. Paper documents have proved more resistant than expected. In fact, print on paper is doing much more than just hanging on. So many new avenues for paper documents continue to develop that we are using more paper than ever. Books in the traditional mode will be with us throughout the 21st century. They are, after all, an elegant user-friendly medium that will not become unreadable when the technology changes.

There are some concerns surrounding electronic books. They are published more quickly and with less editorial oversight, so there is a greater chance for error. Publishers need to ensure that the positive qualities of the paper book system—quality controls, selectivity, and so forth—be maintained in the new environment. Publishing companies have made sure that late 20th century copyright law is applied in the 21st-century e-book context. The notion of a public library where we can all check out books is viewed as an unprofitable relic. Sharing an e-book with a friend is not a likely possibility.

All of this is so new and futuristic that most people have not even begun to consider the social issues that surround the use of such new technology. Lobbyists for the publishing industry, with little public attention, managed to get Congress to pass the Digital Millennium Copyright Act. Now people who use specially designated software to read an e-book are identified every time they read something. It is a publisher's dream: A person who is not authorized to read an e-book is committing a crime. Fortunately, we still have the freedom to read and share paper books.

Because e-books are part of our future (Figure 1-3), we should consider them in a social and educational context. There are some advantages to carrying 50 pounds of books on a Reader that weighs only a couple of pounds. Although it is not superior to a printed book, the e-book opens a range of possibilities for helping readers to master words, passages, and concepts in a new way. When a reader encounters a word that he can't pronounce or a concept that she doesn't understand, the e-book will provide the correct pronunciation and an explanation.

It is unlikely that any electronic media will become the main container of content. E-books are simply one of the new waves of the literary future. They will become one of the many ways that we will use digital tools to read, watch, and investigate. An array of digital products will continue to evolve as they spread across the landscape. An exotic collection of literary hybrids will change how we read, write, and communicate. Already some books have become part of distant databases, allowing readers to extract and combine what they want from pools of digital information.

Electronic Readers make it easier for a book to be customized as it is downloaded from the Internet. When publishers allow books to be reduced to digital pieces, readers pay only for the pages or chapters that they use. The online world is well suited for those who want to buy only specific chapters of a book. It is also possible to chop different books up into interchangeable parts and allow customers to buy a highly targeted text. This customization is made possible by online services like IDG and iUniverse. Publishers have farmed out some of their titles to these and other companies with online digital systems that allow readers to assemble and pay for the specific pieces they want.

Figure 1-3. E-Books: Here Today, More tomorrow.

When it comes to teaching the language arts, technology is an important tool, but it is not the only tool. It takes caring and capable teachers to change schools for the better. Once the pedagogical piece is in place, we can figure out how technological tools like electronic books can help us to achieve our instructional goals.

In and out of school, avoiding the most powerful information and communication technologies of our time is not an option. There are plenty of entrepreneurs out there who would like to set things up for us. If we let them, they will be happy to impose their version of the future on us. A better arrangement is for the American public, educators, and policy makers to exert some control over the vested interests and the rough edges that surround new technologies. As far as the schools are concerned, this means being proactive about how the instructional environment is being constructed. The future is, after all, not just some place that we are going to; it is also one that all of us should be involved in creating.

Visual Imprinting in Children

Each type of medium has its own agenda and does best with its own kind of content and particular orientation. The advantage to the electronic variety is that it can be an exciting visual introduction to worlds that would otherwise go unseen. Potentially this could provide the highest form of justice to the visible universe.

Children retain certain kinds of material presented by visually intensive media and tend to comprehend more of what they see than what they read or what they hear on the radio or on audiotape—and they remember it longer. The learning style of the child affects the degree to which visual media influences comprehension, but the direction of that influence is constant. In general, children are more attracted to action and sound effects than to dialogue. Once that action is viewed, it tends to be remembered.

Any medium that provides access to millions of minds has the latent ability to extend literate thought. Unfortunately, because of the commercial nature of American mass media, tapping the possibilities has always been difficult. The fact that a new medium like the Internet is taking on commercial television values speaks volumes about the influence of television on any promising new medium in America.

Television and its younger associates may promote different mental skills than those developed by reading and writing, but these skills are not automatically inferior to those developed by print media. TV's wide accessibility has the potential for making certain kinds of learning available for groups of children who do not perform well in traditional classroom situations. In addition, television can reach children on their home ground. To deal intelligently with that home invasion, however, requires critical study in the classroom. Excluding any medium from analysis places users at a disadvantage.

Television has long been an engaging and deserving target for criticism, but many of the same issues, such as violence, extend to film, video games, and the Web. Violence in public entertainment is a lethal American issue. It helps to shape our characters and our lives. Everyone seems to have an opinion about the profusion of violence in the media, but paralysis sets in when it comes to doing much about it. Resolving such dilemmas will require private individual measures and large-scale collective efforts. Whatever the programming, however, critics agree that it has a certain harsh power that is very compelling for large numbers of people.

The developmental aspects of how children learn and process information should guide the programming of different media forms. Research on children's educational TV programs has found, for instance, that visually dramatic techniques can be extremely useful in teaching early reading skills. It would be interesting to find out if the same holds true across other types of electronic media. Children are easily taken by the video screen, which can act as a powerful agent of socialization. It has also been found that children very easily discover their creativity and are able to visually articulate and restructure subject matter concepts with the help of quality educational programming.

From e-mail to the Internet, we have to learn how to manage electronic tools carefully or they will take control of our time. Digital technologies may be reshaping the way education is practiced, but learning requires active social involvement and personal mental effort. New educational programs can get children actively involved by sending their school (or parents) closely related computer programs and print media. Each medium stands alone yet relates to the same teaching concept. Innovative educational programming can play to the strength of electronic media and even redefine the boundaries of television, computers, and print media (Figure 1-4).

The video screen is where the majority of Americans view movies, but whether on the theater screen or on the TV set, the dynamics of film are a bit different. The production values are higher, with cameras, lighting, and sound arranged differently. Why is there so much sex and violence in movies these days? It used to be that movie studios made most of their money in the United States; now they make more overseas. Action pictures are more direct and easier to translate than comedies or dramas. Strong character development, dialogue, and comedy hang on a thin cultural thread.

Technology: The Key to Unlocking True Engagement

There has been a greater realization and acceptance of the necessity of developing positive attitudes toward lifelong learning. Education is still prized as the primary vehicle for realizing the potential of human faculties and socioeconomic improvement. Even though America's dissatisfaction with its dominant information medium (television) and its dominant educational institution (schools) has been chronic, faith in education—and now in technological solutions as well—continues. There are a few things we are certain about concerning the future. We know that

Figure 1-4. Poorly implemented technologies trap students
in false representations of life and the world.

children will learn at a much earlier age and that education will be powered by technology. We also know that learning is a life-long adventure that will take place more often in nontraditional settings such as the home, the workplace, the natural habitat, and even in outer space. Technology will play an increasingly critical role in overcoming geographic and time barriers that have given learning a sequential and linear mode, which is now clearly outdated. Far more important than technology, however, is the human teacher, who will continue to drive and direct this push toward technology-enhanced learning experiences in uncharted waters.

A major goal of education is to motivate students to continue to learn, to discover out of sheer interest, and to be more adventurous in the world of ideas. Tributary goals include instilling the desire to read, speculate, think differently, deduce new insights, propose new interpretations, and be open to the possibility of being filled with wonder and irony. Technological tools need to be played with in uncovering frameworks upon which to hang ideas. Technology should be used to help feed an unsatiated hunger for learning that should last a lifetime.

Technology can be used to override the limitations placed upon us by learning in the physical world as we know it. Although concrete, direct experiences in the actual environment provide the best means of teaching children, these real experiences may not be available all the time; practice may be needed first, or the subject may be too distant in time and space. Here is where technology steps in. Electronic media can help students to go beyond seeing and hearing to provide opportunities for firsthand learning. With a carefully prepared agenda and when properly used, computers conjure dazzling electronic imagery, concoct clever simulations, and facilitate Internet surfing trips that know no bounds. What's found on the street is not necessarily always the best teacher. Concrete experience does not hold the only key to reality. In a good movie, for instance, reality is frequently a cleverly disguised illusion. Whatever the subject, the human construction of reality is to some degree an invention. An inventive novelist might distort the facts to get at the truth. In a play, exaggeration might be put to the same task.

The use of technological tools presents a new set of challenges, however. Although it's exciting to behold how technology engages students to the point that they do more work on a project simply because it's fun, it's equally critical to ask if, in fact, what they're learning is important. Teachers will continue to be relied upon as the prime designers of quality instructional programming and architects of curriculum-based electronic learning environments. Content and pedagogy will not become less important with the influx of technological tools. On the contrary; without intelligent application, even the best electronic media could be rendered ineffective.

Chalk on the blackboard is giving way to pixels on a screen. In some school districts, field trips now come with digital cameras, laptop computers, and the technological capacity for downloading the material onto school computers for multimedia reports. Multimedia computers with moving video and good graphics certainly spice up a dry subject, but many students get nowhere near the technological possibilities. Access usually depends on a community's wealth and on knowledgeable teachers. In America, excellence doesn't always connect to equity.

A Sharper Eye for New Media Visual Fare

Technologically empowered classrooms also leave a lot of room for designing lessons around the individual needs and complexities of real youngsters living in a real world. Research has shown that when the learner is given decision-making authority under the guidance of a knowledgeable adult, genuine engagement takes place. We are very much at the stage in which more intellectual autonomy could be unleashed well beyond chalk, talk, and work sheet. Just as clearly, adult attention discretely applied can encourage children to grow.

Discussion over the place of the "old" and "new" literacies in the curriculum is a vital debate. The struggle is between worthy opponents contending for a larger share of the pedagogical picture. The central question is what fraction of instructional time will be spent with which communication medium. One thing is certain: Visual literacy will be more important than ever.

Visual literacy might be thought of as the ability to comprehend and create visuals in a variety of moving and static media in order to communicate effectively. This involves components of writing, reading, comprehension, visual interpretation, critical evaluation, and production. Images have always been important to learning and its transfer to real-world situations. New technology just amplifies the process.

There's nothing new about the power of the visual image. From cave drawings to medieval cathedrals to children's book illustrations, visual imagery has been a major human communication tool. What's new is the ability of technologically enhanced tools to amplify its impact. Electronic versions of illustrations, photographs, charts, and graphs can increase children's learning of meaningful written and verbal material. Visual thinking and visual rehearsal are effective instructional techniques. Teaching with images can help students to focus on lessons, retain information, and improve psychomotor skills. Children who view illustrations of a story may well recall more of it than students who just listen to it being read. Illustrations and their internal representation can improve retention and comprehension.

Being a Discriminating Consumer of New Media Content

The advent of multimedia and broadband-based technologies has resulted in a number of stunning developments. Television, computer programs, and the Internet grow more visually striking and interactive with each passing year. Netcams now let us see whom we are dealing with on the Internet. New digital technology allows cameras to view things previously seen only with devices like electron microscopes or radio telescopes. The digitization of one picture allows the viewer to zoom in or provide three-dimensional imagery of the elements from any angle. Computer graphics and simulation can take over from there. Students can "see" what it's like to be in the middle of an atom or looking at the galaxy, where no camera or science, for that matter has previously gone. In a digital environment, the supremacy of physical proximity is no longer omnipotent.

Youngsters can sometimes get closer to understanding with electronic devices than they can with books or through discussion. This is especially true if electronic imagery is coupled with concrete activities. Simulate a dangerous chemical reaction, and then use some real chemicals for something safer. Actual chemical experiments can be viewed at the micro level with new digital cameras and graphically simulated by computer, but the technology only takes us so far. Computer-mediated online study can teach many things. However, learning the broader themes of life requires a certain amount of face-to-face interaction with knowledgeable adults and a community of peers. Classrooms that are centered on learners and learning recognize the importance of interpersonal dialogues, critical thinking, and active collaboration.

Mass communication is the production and distribution of messages with technological devices. Although there are some new kids on the block, certain principles still hold. Becoming a critical consumer of any medium requires training. Multiple media platforms can mount programs that can entertain us, distract us, or implant worthy concepts in our hearts and minds.

Being an intelligent consumer of media implies an understanding of the form and content of media messages. It also implies an understanding of how to place those messages in a context and of how the various social, political, and commercial forces shape the message. Media literacy involves critical viewing skills and the ability to examine, evaluate, and interpret content. Teachers, parents, and others can take this neglected literacy and develop serious learning activities.

Using Technology for Designing Interactive Learning and Connectedness in the Classroom

The Internet has been praised as superior to television and other passive media because it allows users to choose the kind of information they want to receive and, often, to respond to it in chat rooms, e-mail exchanges, or on electronic bulletin boards. The reality is that sometimes we connect and sometimes we don't. It has long been known that television reduces social involvement. The idea that Internet communications can be just as lonely may come as a surprise to many, but virtual relationships can be disembodied and distant when formed in the vacuum of cyberspace.

The problem with much of our current information and communication technology is that it can fill our heads with isolated fragments of facts without providing the social context that would give these facts meaning. This can make life in the world's technological societies a whirl of disconnected general notions and attitudes. Fortunately, there are some positive possibilities. For example, teachers can avoid placing children in solitary confinement by pairing them up on a computer. No one has to be trapped in the sad, lonely world of cyberspace. Teachers can also take advantage of the computer's proven ability to provide dynamic visual representations of various concepts.

We would do well to remember that the entire curriculum, no matter how advanced technologically, must be filtered through the mind of the teacher. The most comprehensive high-tech curriculum and the most pleasant school environment are of little use unless they are matched by quality teachers. Putting learned thoughts and principles into action requires preparation and sustained professional development.

An effective medium has the ability to change how we use our senses to process thought and perceive reality. Like traditional reading and writing, it is not a simple matter of decoding symbols but also of constructing meaning. The video image is more vivid than print and speaks powerfully to a new generation. The ease with which the electronic image involves all of our senses is unparalleled in the history of communications. On a superficial level it is easier to decode, but deeper understanding and control is harder to come by. When new electronic means are coupled with effective teaching strategies, speech, writing, print, and visual media can all be enhanced.

The use of technology isn't about getting away from reading and writing. It's about giving the student a richer, more interactive experience that enhances basic education. Eventually, all successful media become transparent as we lose consciousness of the medium itself and think about what truth it has told us about ourselves and our world. No matter how powerful the technology, learning how to write well, communicate with team members, and speak effectively in public will be part of what we do in school.

Just as the computer has changed our relationship to television, the Internet is changing our relationship to both. We are starting to get good enabling programs that allow us to sort through the glut of information, but unlocking the full potential of communication and information technology is beyond the tech-nological horizon in education. One thing is certain: Within the next few years a powerful new media synergy will radically change how we think and how we learn.

There is general agreement that information and communi-cation technology can help us to reexamine instructional strate-gies and educational goals. It is just as clear that digital media is becoming increasingly important in education. The various stan-dards projects recognize these developments and point to the need for incorporating electronic media into the core curricu-lum. Certainly electronic media is becoming a dominating agency of education throughout the world. What isn't clear is exactly how technology will improve instruction and change the day-to-day work of teachers.

Media experiences both inside and outside the classroom can provide access to learning for all students. Our shared media culture can serve as the basis for classroom exploration. The critical factor is always how the technology is used by people, but there is no reason that we can't turn the one-way commer-cial system of mass media into a two-way process of reflection and discussion. Creative action with one another and with the media itself is key.

By applying their knowledge of effective instruction and us-ing high-tech tools, teachers can help children to imagine, cre-ate, and reach new thinking and learning plateaus. By using the technological tools of the day and the intellectual tools of their profession, teachers can open student minds to subject matter and the potential of promising technology.

The Technology Piece
of the Literacy Puzzle

> Our inventions should be more than an improved
> means to an unimproved end.
>
> —Henry David Thoreau

In the 21st century, individuals must be highly literate, flex-ible, and capable of identifying and solving problems. The days of a highly educated elite and a general population with basic skills are over. Computer-based technology can do most of the repetitive tasks. To remain competitive in a rapidly changing world, societies now have to make sure that the majority of their citizens are well educated. This will require clear, high standards for all students. It will also require a sustained societal focus with clearly recognizable consequences when those standards are not met. Once we have the means and the will, all of our citizens can be educated to their fullest potential. Nothing would be more wonderful for the individual and for the community in which we must all live together.

Technology does not have a magical ability to turn things around educationally. It should never be a destination, but it can be an effective vehicle for opening multiple paths to many subjects. Putting learning and the full human component first is key to its effective use. The challenge is learning how newer media can be understood, how it can improve instruction, and how it can help to shape a better future.

Technological possibilities provide one set of lenses; our expanding knowledge of human beings provides another. Neuroscience and cognitive psychology are expanding our understanding of how humans learn. As far as technology is concerned, the complexity imposed by software is fading, and it is getting easier to use. Who knows what will take the place of the information age as the 21st century progresses? No matter how literacy evolves, children will always need real teachers for companionship on journeys of discovery and enlightenment.

At the same time that the teacher's role is becoming more complex, working conditions and poor pay have led to a dangerous shortage of talented people in the teaching profession. The schools need a fresh infusion of thoughtful and generous adults who want students to see, think, know, and perform better.

Practical Guidelines for Classroom Cyber Tours

This section includes practical tips for teachers in designing electronic, online "discovery journeys" for their students in using the Internet and the World Wide Web.

- It's very easy for students to get lost in "solitary confinement" in cyberspace. To prevent this, make sure your students work in a computer workstation in the school's computer lab with at least one other "buddy." Advise parents to keep the family computer in a commonly shared area such as the living room, home library, reading room, or family room. Design Web-surfing homework for your students that will require the participation of parents, brothers, sisters, or others in exciting interactive exercises.
- Spend some time in the classroom clarifying values that revolve around decent and appropriate learning material.

Very discreetly point out what constitutes "offensive" material, give concrete examples, and delicately explain the dangers of seeking and exposing oneself to "low-grade" online Web sites.

- Advise the parents of your students to use "parental control tools" to streamline and select what your students can view online. As a teacher in the classroom, you can also use these same tools in configuring Web sites that you intend your students to work with in class. These tools provide "safe areas" for children, rating systems for evaluating Web sites, search engines to assist in finding information previously approved for family viewing, and so forth. Parents and teachers should evaluate these tools according to the following features: (a) appropriateness of the protection measures for the family concerned; (b) compatibility of the tool with the family's home computer system; (c) reasonableness and affordability of subscription or one-time fees imposed by the Internet service providers or software manufacturers; and (d) accessibility of the tool through the use of popular commercial Internet service providers. For more information see http://www.childrens partnership.org/pub/pbpg98/partII98.html#findplaces.

- Caution your students to be careful in their retrieval and use of information posted on various Web sites. Although information is plentiful, it isn't necessarily accurate, reliable, or substantive. Explain to students that the nature of the organization sponsoring the site largely affects the motivation behind posting certain types of information. Commercial sites, for instance, are adept at designing "infomercials" that make advertising text appear like neutral and objective information postings. Direct your students toward the use of noncommercial, nonprofit educational sites that do not promote the sale of products or services. For more information see http://www.ed.gov/pubs/parents/internet/tips.html.

- Train your students to always acknowledge the Web sites from which they cite or quote passages for class work. Encourage them to write or list the names of the Web sites and their respective uniform resource locators (URLs) so that others can visit these sites as well. For more information see http://www.ed.gov/pubs/parents/internet/tips.html.

- Do not be surprised if organizations, Web sites, or companies know how to find you or your students on the Web.

Internet-based technologies such as "cookies" track places you've been on the Internet. This is a piece of software code stored in the hard drive of your computer that carefully records your electronic tracks as you navigate within and across different web sites. The "cookie" feature of your Web browser can be turned off; find out how from your Internet service provider or the Web master of the browser software you are using. Also, it is prudent for you to deal with Web sites that have "e-trust" icons or symbols. These sites will more likely than not leave you alone and not collect information on your manner of exploring their sites. Better yet, work only with educational Web sites that have explicitly stated policies about not gathering confidential information on their visitors without first seeking their permission and not selling information on their Web site users. For more information see www.cais.net/cannon/memos/parents.htm.

- More and more Web sites elicit visitor participation in "chat rooms," which can be very engaging for children. The obvious danger is that adults can pose as children and lure other chat room participants toward unseemly activities. Teachers and parents should remain vigilant in overseeing young students' participation in chat areas, especially in Web sites that are not well known or visibly regulated. E-mail messages to children generated from such chat room participation should be monitored as well. For more information see http://www.kidsonthenet.com/safety/p2.html.

- E-commerce Web sites are a big thing nowadays, a new form of consumerism that feeds instant gratification. Many sites target children and young adults. Consumer sites are also using increasingly enticing interactive marketing ploys to get young consumers to purchase as quickly as possible. Teachers can help children to critically deconstruct the codes of advertising and build their knowledge of media messages. Parents can help by monitoring and supervising their children's online purchasing activities. It's also a good idea to keep children away from credit cards and other forms of electronic payment.

Although the impact of digital technology on schools is bound to be immense, its exact form is far from predictable. Techno-enthusiasts often have a kind of tunnel vision that cuts them off from their peripheral field. Human judgment, the educational environment, teacher training, basic habits, social relationships, and institutions all play major roles in how, when, and whether a particular technology is adopted. Remember that the impact that any new device or application is most likely to have is a positive effect if we design the technology, the social systems, and the educational possibilities holistically. The intelligent use of technology requires putting educational goals and standards in place before welcoming the technology onslaught.

Literacy and Life in a Digital World

> The future is not some place we are going to,
> but one we are creating. The paths to it are not
> found but made, and the activity of making them
> changes both the maker and the destination.
>
> —John Schaar

E-mail and Web sites are now ubiquitous, and online users total in the hundreds of millions in the United States alone. Every month we see new hardware and software innovations that allow for more and more functionality. As the literacy umbrella spreads to cover information and communication technology, applications multiply and are added to smaller and smaller devices. Wireless users now have access to powerful handheld devices that allow them to closely duplicate the experience of being at home with an online computer. In this age of the euphoric pursuit of information for its own sake, it is easy to forget that information is a means to an end, not an end in itself. With all our whiz-bang technology, it is easy to lose sight of the fact that the development of appropriate ways of relating to others will be a central feature of the social objectives of schooling in the 21st century.

As the schools greet the future, new content-standards curricula encourage teachers to help students critically perceive, analyze, interpret, and discover the range of meanings conveyed by print and nonprint media. In the 21st century, American children will spend many years using and mastering elements of new multimedia literacy systems and learning how to use them flexibly and fluently. They will also continue to achieve literacy through natural social interaction. The difference is that they will create and communicate meanings and actively use all kinds of digital media. Making the best use of available media is a constant juggling act that requires a respect for the inherent values of all modes of communication.

Schools cannot avoid the electronic juggernaut that is plowing through today's world. If educators do not attend to the most powerful multimedia technologies of their time, then their professional reality will be shaped by a vision they do not share. Conversely, if educators are proactive participants in building the new knowledge society, then they will play an even more meaningful role in engaging students. The future is, after all, not the result of alternative paths offered by the present. Rather, it a place that is created first in the mind and will, then in activity.

References

Adams, D. M., and Hamm, M. (2000). *Literacy today: New standards across the curriculum.* New York: Falmer Press.

Association for Educational Communications and Technologies and the American Association of School Librarians. (1998). *Information literacy standards for student learning.* Washington, DC: Authors.

Brown, J. S., and Duguid, P. (2000). *The social life of information.* Cambridge, MA: Harvard Business School Press.

Calvert, S. L. (1998). *Children's journeys through the information age.* New York: McGraw-Hill.

Castells, M. (2000). *The rise of the network society.* Oxford, UK: Blackwell.

Catudal, J. N. (2001). *Privacy and rights to the visual: The Internet debate (philosophy and the global context).* Lanham, MD: Rowman & Littlefield.

Coles, R. (1997). *The moral intelligence of children.* New York: Random House.

Cortes, C. (2000). *The children are watching: How the media teach about diversity.* New York: Teachers College Press.

Dertouzos, M. L. (1998). *What will be: How the new world of information will change our lives.* San Francisco: Harper Business.

Dominick, J. R., et al. (1999). *Broadcasting, cable, the Internet and beyond: An introduction to modern electronic media.* New York: McGraw-Hill.

Fox, R. F. (2001). *MediaSpeak.* Westport, CT: Praeger.

Gardner, H. (1999). *The disciplined mind.* New York: Simon & Schuster.

Hamilton, J. T. (1998). *Channeling violence: The economic market for violent television programming.* Princeton, NJ: Princeton University Press.

Harper, C. (1999). *And that's the way it will be: News and information in a digital world.* New York: New York University Press.

Haughland, S. W., and Wright, J. L. (1997). *Young children and technology.* Needham Heights, MA: Allyn & Bacon.

Herman, A., and Swiss, T. (Eds). (2000). *The World Wide Web and contemporary cultural theory: Magic, metaphor, and power.* New York: Routledge.

Kagan, J. (1998). *Three pleasant ideas.* Cambridge, MA: Harvard University Press.

Kaye, B. K., & Medoff, N. J. (1999). *The World Wide Web: A mass communication perspective.* Mountain View, CA: Mayfield.

Kurzweil, R. (1998). *The age of spiritual machines: When computers exceed human intelligence.* New York: Viking.

Levinson, P. (1999). *Bestseller: Wired, analog, and digital writings.* Culver City, CA: Pulpless.Com.

Lipschultz, J. (1999). *Free expression in the age of the Internet: Social and legal boundaries.* Boulder, CO: Westview Press.

McMahon, D. (2000). *Cyber threat.* Toronto, Ontario: Warwick.

Monaco, P. (2000). *Understanding society, culture, and television.* Westport, CT: Praeger.

Moravec, H. (1998). *Robot: Mere machine to transcendent mind.* New York: Oxford University Press.

Negroponte, N. (1995). *Being digital.* New York: Vintage Books.

Owen, B. M. (2000). *The Internet challenge to television.* Cambridge, MA: Harvard University Press.

Rich, D. (1997). *MegaSkills: Building children's achievement for the information age.* New York: Houghton Mifflin.

Sawyer, B., et al. (2000). *Online broadcasting power.* Cincinnati, OH: Muska & Lipman.

Stoll, C. (1995). *Silicon snake oil.* New York: Anchor Books.

Tapscott, D. (1999). *Growing up digital: The rise of the Net generation.* New York: McGraw-Hill.

Todreas, T. M. (1999). *Value creation and branding in television's digital age.* Westport, CT: Quorum Books.

Turkle, S. (1995). *Life on the screen: Identity in the age of the Internet.* New York: Simon & Schuster.

Winston, B. (1998). *Media technology and society: A history from the telegraph to the Internet.* New York: Routledge.

 # Media Production: Storyboards, Video, Computers, and More

---

The key to successful integration of multi-literacies in schooling is to stress the manipulation of technology tools by students, so that they become information providers as well as receivers.

— *Kathleen Tyner*

Media is the physical means through which information may be communicated or aesthetic forms created. To be fully literate in the 21st century, students must be familiar with the newer languages of wider communication. Special attention is given in this book to helping students understand and construct visual environments with electronic media. When students use current technology to create media messages, they come to see the wide range of expression possible within a medium.

Media literacy may be thought of as the ability to create personal meaning from the visual and verbal symbols we take in every day from television, advertising, film, and digital media. It is more than inviting students to simply decode information. They must be critical thinkers who can understand and create in the media culture swirling around them. Being able to identify the capabilities, limitations, and possible combinations of contemporary media is important in approaching the potential of these systems to address personal, educational, and workplace needs. Creating with technological tools motivates students and provides them with feedback that is not possible from pen and paper. Achieving varying levels of literacy in a medium is important, but there are broader implications. The effect of literacy in one area has an impact in another. Having students actively analyze and create knowledge with a mix of media is key to multiple technology-intensive literacies.

Design tasks, like media production, require teachers who are familiar with the principles underlying the characteristics of effective instruction and who are prepared for the mix of media through which these principles can be applied. When technological tools, subject matter, and sound pedagogical principles go hand in hand, they open doors to what all students should know and understand.

Knowledge consists of past constructions that come about through assimilation and accommodation. This constructivist approach to instruction has proven to be a solid foundation for literacy, learning, and media education. Within this framework, learning is viewed as an organic process of invention rather than a mechanical process of accumulation. If new information doesn't fit into an existing logical framework, a higher level of explanation develops. Meaningful learning occurs through reflection and resolution of such cognitive conflict.

Children learn best when they experience things themselves and then have time to think about those experiences as well as what they have seen and done. When children learn about the world through their own activity, thought, and teamwork, they reinforce their natural interests and curiosity. Such collaborative inquiry is one of the core values of constructivist culture and is central to media production. Problem-based team activities work because they expose learners to the thinking of their peers and help them to reconcile instructional experiences with their existing knowledge and the social contexts within which this knowledge occurs.

Learning and the Power of Media Tools

Constructivist learning is more than a set of teaching techniques; it is a pattern of expectations that underlies relationships among teachers, students, and the world of ideas. It is based on the premise that people do not have to be told how to do something. Tell them what to do and give them the tools, and they will exhibit their own ingenuity.

What students can do with others today they can do alone tomorrow. Many teachers, including those who are just beginning to use technology as a tool, like to pair students up on the basis of skill. They put a student who knows about the media involved with one who doesn't. The teacher prepares a simple one-page set of directions that students working together can figure out. Then students row out into the electronic sea. The teacher moves from one small group to another. This strategy provides more motivation than the lecture and textbook method of instruction. Even teachers who are very familiar with the technology often do this because it enhances collaborative inquiry, creativity, and transfer. As students engage in collaborative inquiry, they can experience the media, the concepts, and the nature of literacy in a multimedia age.

From video cameras to editing machines, computer chips seem to be in everything today. Video recordings, motion pictures, computer programs, and the Internet often mix things up to portray subjects with motion and sound. Video is a good starting point. When it is coupled with pacing and a sense of continuity, the video medium is a great way to present information, clarify a complex concept, and tell a powerful story. Visual texts can come in many forms, but all involve a complex dynamic of power and pleasure. The basic concepts of video production apply across visually intensive media. Video can be mixed with sound, text, and computer graphics before being sent out on the Internet. The Internet is proving to be a strange hybrid of print and video media. The convergence of media will continue as everything from WebTV to high-speed methods of Internet access (e.g., cable modems) become more widespread.

As children take part in the problem-solving activities that characterize constructivist classrooms, teachers must be sure that the process of learning by doing doesn't cause students to become primarily manipulators of the medium rather than critical thinkers about the content they are developing and about the power of the media to develop that content. At its best, the manipulation of technology tools (production) goes hand in hand with critical media analysis. Even though students are eager to get on with production, they must be encouraged to look at broader background issues, such as how to achieve the intended visual, informational, and emotional impact. Students need a solid conceptual background in a medium, and they need to understand that all media are constructed and manufactured products with a wide range of commercial, social, and political implications. Reflecting upon the complex interactions among technology, curriculum, and culture is more important than making a video or creating a Web site.

Video Production — A Good Place to Start

The basic concepts of composition, lighting, sound, and planning apply across all visual media. Student can make videos and put them on other technology platforms. It is now possible to transcend physical boundaries by shooting a short video and sharing it online with students around the world. Media can be mixed in many ways — shoot a video, digitize it, and put it on the Web. The Internet changes the cartography of communication by allowing anyone with access to a computer to get his or her work all over the world in days.

For live action, Netcams are easy to set up and even come installed in some of the new laptops. They allow the users to see the person with whom they are communicating. Like most video on the Web, it is a bit choppy, but the technology is steadily improving. One can start and finish with the video production, or at other times move into the digital world with computers, the Internet, and multimedia production.

Children can master the video production process and affect their attitudes toward learning in ways not possible with other media. If students have a camcorder at home, they can teach others how to use it. This way, students can apply previous knowledge and collaborate with peers as they form new knowledge from their learning experiences. When others depend on them, students are motivated because their individual contributions result in a collaboratively produced video. Each member is encouraged to take pride in specializing in a specific step of the video production process.

Student video producers can take advantage of computers to add titles, sound, and graphic designs to the production. Peer reviews of video production can be done much like peer reviews of written stories. Making full-motion video stories is now surprisingly easy. New camcorders have so many features that the production can often all be done without editing equipment. One needs only a TV and a VCR to play it back. Sometimes the VCR is not even necessary because some camcorders can be directly hooked to the TV for playback. The standard videotape cassette is a relatively unstable medium to edit and rapidly degrades with each edit. The advantage to digitized video is that it can be transferred and copied many times without degrading the quality. Off-the-shelf software and a good school computer can create images that rival professional moviemakers of the early 1990s.

Video — Yesterday, Today, and Tomorrow

What the epic poem did for ancient cultures — and the novel for modern literate societies — is now done for most Americans by television. As literature and the arts moved away from our common culture, the mass media moved in. Led by television, the electronic media now permeate almost every facet of our lives.

A few hundred dollars can now buy a camcorder with a 3-inch LCD color monitor that makes it easy to take high- or low-angle shots (seeing exactly what is happening) without going through contortions. In addition, inexpensive camcorders now come with a built-in auto-light that turns on and off as needed and with auto-focus and auto-exposure control. An attractive feature that should be included on the camcorder is digital image stabilization. This feature makes everything look more professional because it smooths out unintentional camera movement (the mark of an amateur). These picture stabilizers compensate for hand-held camera shaking without affecting deliberate pans and tilts. Digital hyper-zoom features now let the user get extra close and control the speed of the zoom with one finger. Digital wipes and fades add to the quality. Using a compact digital camcorder that has all of these features and that can easily be connected to a standard VHS unit allows for playback just about anywhere.

As with using computers, video production has been demystified. Specific techniques that were formally the province of studio professionals are being harnessed for a host of instructional and home purposes. Camcorders are becoming as common as computers in the American household.

Visual Environments — Their Effects on Society

Utter acceptance and adulation of technology have always been an American hubris, and one that courts disaster. Delving into this characteristic of our society is beyond the scope of this book. To get at such a broad issue would require a perspective deeply informed by history, philosophy, psychology, and literature—a task best left to others. However, a few reference points are useful before diving into the construction of media products.

In the 1950s and 1960s, children grew up being socialized and entertained by television. Although the impact of television was hidden from view, it was already quietly shaping public beliefs and policy. By the late 1970s, television was being used as an electronic teacher, and it was becoming clear that children and young adults needed a greater understanding of how video images shape ideas. Now the technology has advanced to the point where children can actually "write" with it.

Intelligent television viewing and production are parallel processes. The omnipresent technology allows a large cross-section of Americans to pick up a camcorder and explore the conventions of the medium. Learning the processes involved in visually expressing their thoughts and experiences has the side benefit of helping students to become more intelligent consumers of television. Although the focus was traditionally on the three Rs, teachers have always taught students how to interpret and use media message systems. Since visually intensive electronic messages have become the most common mode of mass communication in today's world, it would seem to be a natural part of the school curriculum.

When students learn to use the technology as an extension of themselves, they take a measure of control over a medium that dominates their communications environment. As with any human artistic or learning endeavor, there is an inescapable requirement of experience and background. Creating with television media does require some knowledge and skill in basic video production techniques. Anyone can pick up a camcorder and get some pictures, but to do it well also requires some understanding of visual composition and enough technical knowledge to properly use sound, music, lighting, editing, and camera angles to make your point.

The Storyboard

A storyboard (Figure 2-1) is a visual sketch of how things will happen in a production. There are a variety of approaches to storyboarding, but a well-done video is based on the creation of a storyboard that will be used to guide the production of the video. Table 2-1 provides students with information and tips on creating a useful storyboard.

Table 2-1. Creating a Storyboard

A storyboard is a guide to develop and film a video.
Storyboards can be:
- a cartoonlike scene sequence depicting a story
- a written script
- a computer-generated sequence (using a software program)
- sketches of individual frames on sheets of paper in a looseleaf notebook

Storyboards show:
- placement of characters
- camera angles
- plans for lighting
- plans for sound
- sequence of scenes

The goal of a storyboard is to help the production team answer these questions:
- What is the story about?
- What is the sequence of the action?
- Who are the characters?
- Where are they placed in the scene?
- With whom are the characters in conflict?
- What is the problem? the solution?
- What is the setting? What should be in the foreground, middle ground, and background?
- How should the lighting and sound (including music) be arranged?
- What camera angles and colors should be in each frame?
- What types of set, costumes, and makeup are required?

Tips for developing the storyboard
- Keep a sketch book or looseleaf notebook as production begins.
- Write captions under the pictures or notes on the sides.
- Begin the storyboard with about six frames on a page.
- Use the frames to show the placements of characters, camera angles, light, sound, and sequence of scenes.
- A good storyboard should have at least 10 to 15 frames.

There are computer programs to help screenwriters develop storyboards. Some that college students like to use are Plots Unlimited (by Ashleywilde), Writepro (Writepro Corporation), and Dramatica Pro (Screenplay Systems). Most are too complicated for elementary students, but the techniques described in Table 2-1 can serve as a guide for them. One of the key elements in developing storyboards is the quality of the collaboration among the members of the production team.

Storyboards are used to illustrate individual frames or sequence in everything from television commercials to Web sites to feature films. Alfred Hitchcock, for example, is said to have personally laid out a storyboard for every frame of his films and television productions. Steven Spielberg, Francis Ford Coppola, and just about everyone else in television and movie production uses some type of storyboard.

The storyboard illustrates a series of shots in a logical, structured rhythm reminiscent of action comic strips. It provides an

Figure 2-1. A Storyboard

initial story structure and visual narrative. Table 2-2 provides a suggested activity that will develop students' storyboarding skills.

Table 2-2. Developing Storyboarding Techniques

- Select a commercial on television to watch.
- Count the number of shots used.
- Make a storyboard for the 15- or 30-second commercial.
- Repeat this activity for a sequence from a film or television show.

Simple Production Techniques for Students

Understanding video production helps across all media. Developing students' abilities to use camcorders is key to success in video production. To help children get familiar with the equipment, one technique is to allow children to work in small groups and simply use trial and error as they learn to use a camcorder. If the teacher is not familiar with the equipment, another approach is to assign four or five interested students who have camcorders at home to teach small groups of students a few basic techniques. Another successful approach is to check out the school camcorders to a group of underachieving students and challenge them to learn about the equipment and then teach others. Sometimes it works for children in the upper elementary grades to teach students in lower grades to use the equipment. The best approach to helping students develop their media production skills is through peer teaching and collaborative inquiry.

Before any work with the camcorder begins, students need to think, plan, and visualize what they will shoot. A good starting point is simply to ask students to write a short scene about some situation that makes them laugh, cry, or get angry. Encourage students to be thorough, because scenes that are well thought out are easier to film. Challenge them to treat one concept at a time and to introduce their topic immediately. Help them to break subjects into clearly defined sections and plan how the viewer will become involved. Writing an outline can help accomplish these goals and can also help to determine how long each scene will be. The storyboard serves as a support structure for their work.

Students can improve the quality of their video productions by examining quality television programs, films, photographs, and paintings to understand how visual artists do things such as heighten the intensity of an image with light. It is also helpful if students learn about frame composition. Good visual arts lessons and tours of art museums to reflect on how artists "frame" a subject help students to develop a better understanding of frame composition. This knowledge forms the basis for developing skill with the camcorder. One difficulty students have is figuring the zone of coverage and how the camera and people should move. Table 2-3 provides tips on using a camcorder.

Table 2-3. Tips on Using a Camcorder

- Hold the camera steady.
- Mount the camera on a tripod if possible.
- Brace yourself against a tree, a fence, or someone's shoulder.
- Learn how to move the camera.
- Move the camera slowly.
- Move the camera up or down, right or left, but not in both directions in the same shot.
- Don't move the camera unless there is a good reason to do so.
- Move the camera in a horizontal direction for a panoramic, or "pan," shot.
- Move the camera up or down for a tilt shot.
- Start with a long shot (to establish where the action is taking place) and then zoom in.
- Pay attention to the light source and to shadows in deciding how to shoot a scene.
- Practice moving the camera for pan, tilt, and zoom shots.

Figure 2-2 shows another sample storyboard.

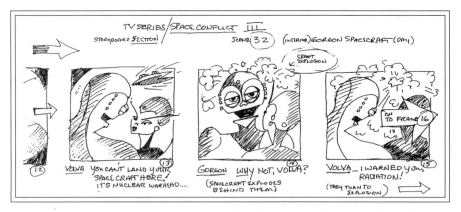

Figure 2-2. Storyboard concepts: Sketches for a TV Series Entitled *Space Conflict III*.

Table 2-4 describes other production techniques that will help students improve the quality of their video productions.

Table 2-4. Choosing Production Techniques

The production techniques that are chosen will determine the impact of the video.

Learn to:
- stop and start action
- bridge sharp changes between scenes
- allow visual action to carry the scene
- use sound as a motivator
- pace the production

Use lighting to clarify the setting and project the desired atmosphere.
1. Striking a balance between light and dark provides the illusion of a three-dimensional space.
2. A keylight can be set up in front of, over, or even under a subject. An underlight has a sinister effect.
3. A backlight can define depth and distinguish a character or object from the background.
4. Fill lights often soften a scene or in long shots pick up background details.
5. "Soft" lighting creates a diffused illumination, whereas "hard" lighting creates clearly defined shadows.
6. Natural light from a door or window can make a scene better.
7. Light quality, direction, source, and color controls the look and function of a scene.

Plan the action on the screen:
1. Rhythm is the series of steps that form successive stages and is decided upon by changing the intensity pattern of the scenes.
2. Pacing is the human interaction or range of emotions.
3. Viewpoint is the position the viewer takes in relation to what is going on.
4. Framing is the balance or symmetry in a frame. The subject of a frame should rarely be placed in the center of the frame, but rather should be positioned to the right or left or just slightly off-center.

cont.

Plan the dialogue, sound, and music

1. Dialogue should consist of short exchanges.
2. Sometimes use thought or physical action to reveal the character or situation instead of the spoken word.
3. Sound can express emotion, mood, and can draw the viewer's attention to detail.
4. Music can advance action in a scene, link dialogue, and explain what is happening.
5. Sound is usually added in the post-production phase.
6. Use a lapel pin microphone or a shotgun microphone placed a foot and a half in front of a speaker to achieve a good quality of sound.
7. Vary the sound levels to add drama.
8. Use "sound bridges" to create transitions from scene to scene.
9. Be aware of noises from air conditioners, metal rubbing against metal, and clothing rustling. These kinds of noises will be much louder on the videotape.
10. To help develop skill in using sound, view professional videos and practice answering these questions:
    - What sounds are present — street noise? music? How loud is it? How does it change?
    - Does the sound come from its visually perceived source?
    - Is the sound happening before, after, or with the story action?
    - Is the sound related rhythmically to the image, like a music video?
    - How do the types of sounds identify function in the video?

Editing the Production

Editing is just as important in film or video as it is in print. The editing process can change the viewpoint and meaning of the video. It also influences the rhythm, mood, visual presentation, and the smooth and logical sequence of a production. One goal of editing is to amplify the narrative in a way that enables the viewer to relate what's happening on the screen to events, dialogue, or situations previously viewed.

The process of editing involves the coordination of one shot with the next. It is the key to the form, construction, and effect of a video. Even first-time video production teams should do their own editing rather than taking their production to Photo-Mat or a small production house. Hands-on editing is essential to ensure that the footage has been used to its best advantage, that good pictorial continuity has been achieved, and that the goals of the project have been met. The editing equipment for beginners using camcorders is inexpensive and no more difficult to operate than loading the camera, setting the exposure, and counting the frames. Editing, like writing, requires learning a few of the conventions, looking at how others do it, and practicing the process.

The editing process is made easier if editorial judgment is exercised before shooting. A well-planned storyboard can enhance the quality of editorial judgment. Visualizing the footage before and during shooting and determining that complete footage has been shot are keys to doing a good job of editing. Once editing begins, all superfluous footage should be eliminated. Even well-shot photogenic scenes can have a negative effect if they complicate or throw the tempo of the video off. Placing cut-ins, cutaways, and other shorts in their proper order, as well as matching action, eliminating bad footage, and adjusting tempo are crucial editing decisions.

It is almost impossible to edit videocassettes by cutting and splicing. While audiocassette tapes can be cut and stuck back together, videotapes are more difficult to cut and splice because the images are not a series of linear frames but rather go across the width of the tape at an angle. However, digital video cameras do give precise editing possibilities. While some camcorders allow editing on the unit and make a smooth transfer of scenes to a VCR, most nonprofessional electronic editing of videotape is still done by hooking up the camcorder to a VCR. Nearly all camcorders have connection terminals and the necessary cables. Plugging into the "line input" selector on the VCR to the "line" position enables one to transfer scenes from the camcorder (or another VCR) to the VCR. With a little practice, the playback and recording machines can be started and stopped simultaneously at the beginning and end of each tape segment.

It is essential to plan how editing will be done before shooting begins, because as editing style changes, so does camera style. For example, television studios have traditionally used three cameras and steady, even lighting. This allows for quicker work and sometimes makes it easier to get coverage and do "live" editing. Film production is almost always single-camera work. Single-camera work facilitates mobility and allows for more interesting pictures. For student videos, single-camera work is usually more successful.

The following are descriptions of three different styles of editing:

Classical Hollywood editing: This is the most familiar editing style. It is commonly thought of as shot 1, 2, 3, and so on, or medium shot, long shot, and close-up shot. Close-ups position the viewer where he could never be. Slow motion allows the viewer insight into the mechanics of motion. Music can add drama and emotion.

Mise-en-scene editing: This editing technique involves camera movement. Here one moves the camera rather than making a cut. This style of editing involves long takes in which the actors develop scenes.

Montage editing: This style of editing can be described as a visual language of conflict between images that crash together. This technique, originally developed by Sergei Einstein, is used in many commercials.

Ideas for Student Productions

The following ideas can be used to develop students' technological literacies.

1. *Create a 30- or 60-second advertisement.*

   This can be done in any medium although camcorders are the tool of choice. Have four student actors decide on a product, do a storyboard, practise the scene, and shoot it. Show the video to the whole class and ask for feedback — two things the students liked about it and one thing that could make the video better. More advanced students can create a television advertisement using video techniques such as flashbacks, cuts, and dissolves. Have them demonstrate how these techniques convey messages to consumers.

2. *Design a poetry video.*

   Assign students to write, record, and shoot a poetry video based on their own writing and performance.

3. *View and produce scenes from different perspectives.*

   To understand how music adds texture to a film or video story, view a scene, like the airplane segment from *Out of Africa*, with no sound. Then view it a second time with the sound on. Using camcorders, encourage students to use close-up shots and panning, tilting, and zooming techniques. Then have them add music to the track.

4. *Do jigsaw editing.*
Give students 10 or 12 short segments of video and have them arrange each clip under the following headings: setting, characters, motivation, time, plot, and cause and effect. Based on their classifications, have them design a coherent film or video.

5. *Play a photography guessing game.*
Encourage students to take part in the adventure of acquiring and viewing just about anything in the environment. Start by encouraging them to view objects from a different perspective. Zoom in on an object, hold, tape, and have students guess what it is from the close-up. Then have students shoot their own close-ups for discussion.

6. *Shoot a single scene.*
Using a single scene, see how many different ways you can view that scene. Discuss the effects of camera angle, panning, and zooming techniques.

7. *Use a video camera for storytelling.*
After critically viewing popular programming such as music videos, students can construct their own set of electronic images to go with the music. Indeed, the very act of using a video camera for storytelling can become a personal tool, seeing through the electronic void, helping to open doors to visual and technological literacy.

8. *Create a video time line.*
Videotape a short but telling scene from a common theme in the life of the group. Have the students imagine where their lives fit on the continuum. Describe visually the major elements of the past and what will happen in the future. Use a computer graphics program to print out a long time line. If you want to put it on the Internet, a digital camera is a good choice.

9. *Make 2-minute "Bites."*
Have students work together as a crew, with one member responsible for sound, one for lighting, one for camera work, and one for direction. Tape a community event. Boil it down to a 2-minute "bite." Discuss what similar evening news boil-down techniques do to a story.

10. *Disseminate the production.*

If several student groups are doing a similar short project, hook up two VCRs and record one tape with all the material on it. Take that tape to the cable company and have the company show it on the public access channel. It is important that students share their work with a real audience. Sometimes the audience is the class, and at other times it's the whole community. With digital cameras it is even possible to put things out over the Internet for viewers around the world. We have our students put things on the Web and keep a count of "hits" so that they know others are connecting with their work.

Today's Media, Students, and the Teacher

There is no going back to a literacy world primarily defined by the written word. Communication and information technologies have changed everything, including the face of economic and social institutions. Teachers have to consider the literacy needs of schooling, the workplace, and a diverse democratic culture. As a culture, we must create forms of education that can meet our social needs and weather future technological changes. It may not be all that difficult for teachers to play their part. Many of the skills they already have apply across media. Teachers who are comfortable teaching reading and writing can apply many of the same basic learning principles to electronic media. Elementary school teachers can leave out more complicated suggestions for secondary school teachers.

Media comprehension and production can inform a broad range of technology-related literacies. Are teachers ready? The "Technology in Education 2000" survey results of the current state of technology in U.S. public schools show that about two-thirds of all schools report that their teachers use the Internet for instructional purposes (Market Data Retrieval, 2000). The good news, obviously, is that the majority were open to new possibilities. The bad news was that teaching may be the only line of professional work in which there isn't significant time or money to upgrade skills. This has to change. It is clear that America needs to enhance the skills of inservice teachers, upgrade standards for prospective teachers, and change how we recruit, prepare, retain, and reward professional educators.

For better schools and better teachers, America needs a change in public thinking about the value of teaching. We also need to do something about the number of good teachers leaving the profession because of low pay, poor working conditions, and the lack of professional development opportunities. The whole package is important, but rich professional development opportunities are key to improving and updating what's happening in our schools. There are plenty of good models out there. The problem is reaching most of the teaching staffs in most of America's schools.

New subject-matter standards have already linked content competency to communication and information technology. Textbook companies recognize the changing nature of literacy. Grassroots, educator-led organizations like the Association for Supervision and Curriculum Development are serving as centers of support, collegiality, and information. Workshops, conferences, and publications help. Many school districts are making resources available to teachers and students. Some have made consultants available. To many educators and policy makers, school reform without technology is like the Internet without computers. It seems safe to say that the technology-intensive future of language and literacy may be bumpy, but it doesn't have to be gloomy.

Teaching and Learning in an Information Age

Although teachers have long had a love-hate relationship with mass media, they are increasingly integrating video and media production techniques into the context of their classrooms. Many states now expect students to be able to access, analyze, evaluate, create, and communicate with electronic media. National subject-matter standards also support teaching students how to create media messages with today's technology. New technology standards for different grade levels point to the importance of studying film, video, television news, and advertising. These skills are viewed as essential for learning and constructing meaning in a media-saturated society (Carnegie Council on Adolescent Development, 1996).

The nature of mass media can provide a powerful entry point to meaningful experiences in the classroom for all students. Being able to create in a given visual medium is becoming almost as important as being able to write in a print culture. The primary goal is not just self-expression or vocational readiness. Hands-on production can lead to informed analysis and give students a degree of creative power as they approach the dominant media of our time. "Reading" and "writing" with electronic media

are becoming as important to literacy in today's world as traditional reading and writing.

Media and Literacy

Choice, control, and forming new knowledge from learning
experiences are key to the intelligent use of any medium. Constructing and reorganizing knowledge are always better than simply assimilating information from the teacher or a textbook. Media
users and creators are at an advantage if they are able to
collaboratively apply previous knowledge to something they want
to learn. Process skills like observing, sorting, comparing, sequencing, measuring, and communicating all help to define the
dimensions of media design and development. Using media in
the classroom does the following:

* helps students to visualize problems and solutions
* engages learners through production work
* supports collaborative inquiry
* increases the perception of control
* links to information sources
* helps to unify curriculum content
* increases teacher productivity

Teaching, learning, and literacy are taking on new meaning
in a multimedia world. Computers and their associates are becoming a powerful medium for information, communication, and
storytelling. The interactive cinematic narrative made possible
by new digital media give us multiple possibilities for a new genre
of literature. Multimedia computers and online communication
also have an immense capacity for helping us to dynamically
explore the physical, biological, social, and cultural world. No
medium provides ultimate answers, but electronic media, at their
best, enhance understanding and open the mind's eye to a sense
of mystery and wonder.

Although the schools may have been a little slow in embrac-
ing technology, now the educational use of information and communication technology is spreading faster than any other form
of curricular change. In some cases it has been a catalyst for
change. There is no longer any question about whether these
tools will be integrated into the life of the school. Now the question is when and how new media energies influence literacy and
learning. Clearly, the human dimension is more important than
all of our magical high-tech instruments. As educators incorporate the latest media into the schools, they must do everything

possible to make sure that the technology builds upon the bonds between human beings and enhances the human spirit.

References

Agnew, W. (Ed.). *Standards-based language arts curriculum: A focus on performance.* Boston: Allyn & Bacon.

Bazalgette, C., & Buckingham, D. (Eds.). (1995). *In front of the children: Screen education and young audiences.* London: British Film Institute.

Begleiter, M. (2000). *From word to image: Storyboarding & the film making process.* Studio City, CA: Wiese, Michael Productions.

Bertelsmann Foundation (Ed.). (1995). *School improvement through media in education.* Gutersloh, Germany: Bertelsmann Foundation.

Birkerts, S. (1994). *The Gutenberg elegies: The fate of reading in an electronic age.* New York: Fawcett Columbine.

Booker, K. (1999). *Film and the American left.* Westport, CT: Greenwood.

Brook, J., & Boal, I. (Eds.). (1995). *Resisting the virtual life: The culture and politics of information.* San Francisco: City Lights Books.

Buckingham, D. (1994). *Children talking television: The making of television literacy.* Philadelphia, Pennsylvania: Falmer Press.

Buckingham, D., & Sefton-Green, J. (1996). *Cultural studies goes to school: Reading and teaching popular media.* Philadelphia, Pennsylvania: Taylor & Francis.

Carnegie Council on Adolescent Development. (1996). *Great transitions: Preparing adolescents for a new century.* New York: Carnegie Corporation of New York.

Coley, R. J., Cradler, J., & Engel, P. K. (1997, May). *Computers and classrooms: The status of technology in U.S. schools.* Princeton, NJ: Educational Testing Service.

Cradler, J. (1995). *Summary of current research and evaluation findings on technology in education.* San Francisco: WestEd.

Davies, J. (1996). *Educating students in a media-saturated culture.* Lancaster, PA: Technomic.

Duncan, B., D'Ippolito, J., McPherson, C., & Wilson, C. (1996). *Mass media and popular culture* (version 2). Toronto, Ontario, Canada: Harcourt Brace.

Ferrell, W. K. (2000). *Literature and film as modern mythology.* Westport, CT: Praeger.

Fraioli, J. (2000). *Storyboarding 101: A crash course in professional storyboarding.* Studio City, CA: Wiese, Michael Productions.

Gee, J. P. (1996). *Social linguistics and literacies: Ideology in discourses.* Cambridge, MA: Harvard University Press.

Godwin, M. (1998). *Defending free speech in the digital age.* New York: Times Books.

Golgen, J. M. (2000). *Storymaking in elementary and middle school classrooms: Constructing and interpreting narrative texts.* Mahweh, NJ: Erlbaum.

Greenfield, P. M., & Cocking, R. R. (1996). *Interacting with Video.* Norwood, NJ: Ablex.

Hart, J. (1998). *The art of the storyboard: Storyboarding for film, TV, & animation.* Newton, MA: Butterworth-Heinemann.

Hoffman, D. D. (1999). *Visual intelligence: How we create what we see.* New York: Norton.

Hischak, T. (1999). *The American musical film song encyclopedia.* Westport, CT: Greenwood.

Kieran, M. (1999). *Media ethics.* Westport, CT: Praeger.

Lewis, M. (1999). *A Silicon Valley story.* New York: Norton.

Linder, L. (1999). *Public access television.* Westport, CT: Praeger.

Lynch, A. (1996). *Thought contagion.* New York: Basic Books.

Market Data Retrieval (2000). *Technology in Education 2000.* Shelton, CN: MDR (A company of the Dun & Bradstreet Corp.). http://www.Schooldata.com/publications3.html.

Meyrowitz, J. (1985). *No sense of place: The impact of electronic media on social behavior.* New York: Oxford University Press.

Negroponte, N. (1995). *Being digital.* New York: Random House.

Piaget, J., & Inhelder. B. (1999). *The child's conception of space.* New York: Routledge.

Popp, J. (1999). *Cognitive science and philosophy of education: Toward a unified theory of learning and teaching.* San Francisco: Caddo Gap Press.

Rawlings, G.J.E. (1996). *Moths to the flame.* Cambridge, MA: MIT Press.

Simon, M. (2000). *Storyboards: Motion in art.* Newton, MA: Butterworth-Heinemann.

Silverblatt, A. (1995). *Media literacy: Keys to interpreting media messages.* Westport, CT: Praeger.

Taylor, B. & Graves, M. F. (2000). *Reading for meaning: Fostering comprehension in the middle grades.* New York: Teachers College Press.

Tufte, E. R. (1997). *Visual Explanations.* Cheshire, CT: Graphics Press.

Turkle, S. (1995). *Life on the screen: Identity in the age of the Internet.* New York: Simon & Schuster.

Tyner, K. (1998). *Literacy in a digital world.* Mahwah, NJ: Erlbaum.

Wallach, L., Dorfman, L., Jernigan, D., & Themba, M. (1993). *Media advocacy and public health: Power for prevention.* Newbury Park, CA: Sage.

Wexelblat, A. (Ed.). (1995). *Virtual reality: Applications and explorations.* New York: Academic Press.

Zettl, H. (1990). *Sight, sound, motion: Applied media aesthetics* (2nd ed.). Belmont, CA: Wadsworth.

 # Collaborative Inquiry: Working Together to Accomplish Shared Goals

---

Language makes us human

Literacy makes us civilized

Technology makes us powerful

The arts add resources for thoughtfulness
  and enlightenment

Inquiry gives us intellectual tools for making
  sense of the world

And being in community with others can make
  us free.

Inquiry is sometimes thought of as the way people study the world and propose explanations based on the evidence they've accumulated. It involves actively seeking information, truth, and knowledge. When collaboration is added to the process, it helps to build the positive relationships that are at the heart of a learning community. Collaborative inquiry may be viewed as a range of concepts and techniques for enhancing interactive questioning, investigation, and learning. When questions that connect to student experience are raised collectively, ideas and strengths are shared in a manner that supports the cooperative search for understanding. By placing the social context closer to the center of their instructional planning, teachers can more effectively encourage inquiry into the big questions that cut across disciplines.

New technology formats often require a more collaborative approach than do traditional media. Teachers can help by setting standards for group work and giving individual tests or orally quizzing group members at random. Individual students can learn social skills such as staying with the group, encouraging participation, elaborating, and providing polite critical analysis. Successful teams arrange things so that each individual feels responsible for doing a fair share of the work. They also do some assessment of both individual and group work. A simple way to do this is to simply have students list two things that they and their group did well and one thing that they and their group could do better.

By promoting social processes and facilitating inquiry technology we enhance and amplify knowledge acquisition. Information and communication technology can encourage active participation by facilitating learning through interactive group mediation. The computer, for example, can become a mediation tool that acts as a competent tutor and a helpful peer. Like its video and Internet associates, computers can encourage the development of the intellectual tools needed for lifelong learning. When people are in control, electronic media can speak to individuals in a very personal way. The downside is that the undisciplined use of any media can become a lonely and colossal waste of time. The path taken depends on social interaction and informed consumption.

Promoting Social Skills

> The collaborative investigations that children can
> do together today they can do and apply alone
> tomorrow.
>
> — Lev Vygotsky

Learning is not something that isolated students should have done to them, it is something they should do in association with others. The social context and the way in which different communications are authored affect the understanding, reception, and production of information. The development of technologies and online programs that create a sense of community is a high priority for anyone interested in providing students with new venues for knowledge acquisition. The most useful technologies of the future will amplify teaching and learning by promoting social processes and genuine learning communities. Teamwork skills do not develop automatically. At every stage of collaborative inquiry, teachers should guide, challenge, and encourage student learning.

Teachers can build supportive group environments by explaining collaborative procedures to students, monitoring small-group inquiry, and helping students to assess group effectiveness at the end of an activity. Engaging students in collaborative inquiry also involves putting them in small, mixed-ability groups where they take responsibility for themselves and for each other. Crafting group work that supports learning for all students requires content and activities that support cohesive small groups and meets the needs of individuals. Teachers don't have to do group work all the time; some use a form of cooperative group work about 50% of the time, and others may set aside more time for group work tasks.

Teachers need to understand and foster the intellectual and social nature of inquiry in their classrooms. For any collaborative effort to work well requires the development of certain academic and social skills that support the cooperative process. As group members work together to produce joint work projects, teachers can quietly help students to promote each other's success through sharing, explaining, and encouraging. Collaborative group inquiry can help just about anyone move beyond competitive and individualistic goal structures. As students come to care about one another, the group can provide individuals with academic assistance, personal support, and suggestions for what might be done to improve the overall effort in the future. When we meet and collaborate with other people, we can accomplish shared goals and get the most out of learning and life.

Critical analysis and creative engagement are all part of collaborative inquiry. Other ingredients include making observations, asking questions, gathering data, using technological tools, and communicating the results. As each person brings his or her unique spirit to the collaborative inquiry process, the group takes on enough power to illuminate the consequences of alternative courses of action. Technology is simply a powerful tool that teams of students need to understand and use in their explorations. All of this and more are bound to affect our daily lives and our approach to education.

Setting Up Possibilities for Collaboration

How can teachers use classroom space to connect the major media of our times to collaborative inquiry? We like to combine critical analysis with production. Understanding how to critically analyze and creatively construct is at the heart of media competency. By its very nature, creating with media requires collaboration. However, production tools and the associated time are not a prerequisite for the study of associative electronic culture. Many teachers simply cut back on the amount of print reading required and critically study a film, video production, CD-ROM, or set of Web sites. Constructive interactivity is a prerequisite. A teacher might show a 4-minute video clip once or twice to add to a discussion, but minds quickly shut down with more than 10 minutes of passive video or film.

The arrangement of physical space can enhance any approach to using or studying media. To see how not to do it, look at how the computer lab line-ups of the last century diminished social interaction. Architecture strongly influences our lives by shaping our public and private spaces. The same principle applies to individual classrooms. The way that teachers arrange classroom space and furniture has a strong impact on how students learn. When desks are grouped in a small circle or students sit side by side in pairs, collaborative possibilities occur naturally. Straight rows send a very different message.

A classroom-designed student interaction makes just about anything more interesting. The way teachers design the interior space of the classroom helps to focus visual attention. It also sets up acoustical expectations and can help to control noise levels. Natural lighting, carpets, comfortable corners, occasional music, and computers that are arranged for face-to-face interaction can all help to set the general feelings of well-being, enjoyment, and morale. Classroom management is actually easier if students know that they can't shout across the classroom, but they can speak quietly to one, two, or three others—depending on the size of the small group.

As students engage in collaborative inquiry, they should sit in a face-to-face learning group that is as close together as possible. The more space between groups, the better. From time to time it is important to remix the groups so that everybody gets the chance to work with a variety of class members. The physical arrangement should allow the teacher to speak to the whole class without too much student movement. It is important to make eye contact with every student in every group without anyone getting bent out of shape or moving desks.

Figure 3-1 shows the different roles required in group work.

Technology Lessons From Yesteryear

As the 20th century fades into history, we should remember a few aspects of how it opened and how it closed. It started with equations on Einstein's blackboard and ended with images from the edge of time, caught by the Hubble space telescope and broadcast via the Internet. What has changed and what remains the same? Is the Net, for example, a new way to look at a new world or a new way to look at the same old world? A little more than 100 years ago, H. G. Wells warned that our developing technology was engaging us in a race between education and catastrophe. An extended explosion of knowledge and new devices made the competition between these two a close race. In the 20th century, scientific and technological advances gave humans the capacity and the technological tools to radically transform their environment. Machines heavier than air started hauling us across continents in a matter of hours. The century also saw moving images sent across continents and the nuclei of atoms split to blow up and light up cities. The applications stemming from an understanding of distance, velocity, and mass changed our world forever.

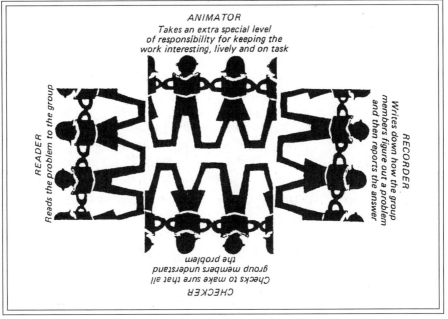

Figure 3-1. Assigning Roles for Group Work

The world seems safer, but catastrophe might still be out there just beyond the horizon. The accidental or purposeful use of nuclear or biological weapons is but one set of horrible possibilities. Global warming is heating up the planet. Of course, some directions may be positive. Toward the end of the 20th century, gene therapy and biotechnology began their march towards revolutionizing medicine and the way humans are put together. The list could go on. Historical analogies are always imperfect, and sometimes they are downright misleading. Still, the old century holds many insights into the directions that technology may take in the early decades of the new century. Before a technology catches on, it commonly goes through several phases.

A basic invention is followed by a period of refinement. To really get things moving, innovations must give people a good reason for adopting the technology. For example, Marconi invented the radio in 1895, but it wasn't until the 1920s that electronic amplification and interesting programming put it into the average American home. The Internet followed a similar curve. It was invented in the late 1960s and used for 20 years by engineers, scientists, and the Defense Department, but it was the 1990s before the World Wide Web and a profusion of visually intensive Web sites got the rest of us interested.

Activities for Discussing Important Technologies

A rank ordering of technology-related activities is a good practical place to start collaborative inquiry into a technology-obsessed world. We randomly surveyed Canadian media and technology experts and came up with an overall priority rating for vital technologies. Table 3-1 shows the results of this study. Whether the ranking is right or wrong is irrelevant. The idea is to get students thinking, talking, and collaborating. When all the groups finish, the teacher can read the answers. Let the students know that the answers aren't absolute and that a survey of different technology experts — or a survey in a different location — would probably order the vital technologies differently. For example, in the sun belt of the United States or in a country like Singapore, air conditioning might be at or near the top of the list. Major social changes, like the status of women, have been left out altogether. Have each group of students rank this mixed order of items, with 1 as most important and 18 as least important.

Table 3-1. The Most Vital Technologies of the 20th Century

movies	airplanes	electricity
cars and trucks	satellites	computers
atomic energy	spacecraft	antibiotics
television	radio	radar
the Internet	biotechnology	telephones
refrigerators	lasers	wireless technology

cont.

Some of these technologies got their start toward the end of the 19th century. Others, like biotechnology, are just starting to show their potential.

Answers: 1. cars and trucks, 2 electricity, 3. airplanes, 4. computers, 5. telephones 6. television, 7. refrigerators, 8. satellites, 9. antibiotics, 10. radio, 11. the Internet, 12. radar, 13. movies, 14. spacecraft, 15. biotechnology, 16. wireless technology, 17. lasers, 18. atomic energy.

Put students into groups of three, four, or five. Everyone comes together to face a challenge. Directions for the students: (a) Rank order the most vital inventions of the 20th century (1 is the most important, 18 the least). (b) Group members try to reach a consensus on their choices and develop a brief rationale for their choices.

If you don't go on to the optional part of the activity, compare each group's answer with the study. Be sure to do at least a little social processing (group self-assessment) at the end.

Optional:

1. Pick a recorder before the group starts to work. The recorder checks off the group behaviors of individuals (see observation checklist). The recorder also uses a tally mark to show how each student in the group performed on each item. Verbal and nonverbal communications are recorded. The recorder has to be an active participant as well.

2. When groups finish their discussions, the teacher can read the ratings of the Canadian media-technology specialists, and the students can compare the difference between their group and the experts.

3. The group evaluates its work and comes up with suggestions for improvement. Students (a) learn how to define and organize work processes, (b) assess the quality of the processes, and (c) sometimes use a quality chart for evaluating effectiveness. Group behaviors that may be assessed include sharing ideas, asking questions, paraphrasing, encouraging and supporting ideas, giving directions, and using appropriate humor.

Groups may be evaluated based on how well members performed as a group. The recorder can go back to the checklist and notes to give individuals specific information about their role in the group.

Checklist and observation form. The teacher uses this checklist to give feedback to the students: Student names, Explaining concepts, Encouraging participation, Checking understanding, and Organizing the work.

4. Another ranking activity is "Big Questions for the 21st Century." Rank your group's view of the importance of some of these issues for the 21st century.
1. Is there a theory that connects everything?
2. Is the expansion of the universe speeding up?
3. Is there a molecular basis of consciousness?
4. What makes us human?
5. How much are we changing the climate?
6. Is there extraterrestrial life?
7. Can we predict earthquakes?
8. Why do we age, and what can be done about it? *Should* anything be done about it?
9. Will blueprints for cells, genes, and DNA yield tailor-made drugs?
10. How will the growth of the Internet affect our lives and our society?

The small sample of scientists we polled suggested the following ranking: 1, 2, 9, 6, 7, 5, 8, 3, 4, 10.

Technological Literacies for a New Century

New communication and information technologies are causing walls to fall all over the world. As digital media takes on a more powerful participatory format, it moves in the direction of sensory presence that can compete for attention with parents, neighborhoods, and schools. In today's multimedia age, human communication continually changes as developers, users, social context, and technology merge and converge.

Worldwide communication and genetic engineering are two of the most powerful technologies shaping our future (Figure 3-2). These diverse fields are starting to overlap as databases of genetic codes move onto the Web. "Bioinformatics" is becoming a hot new field that combines two keystone technologies of the 21st century. The arcane secrets of genetics and molecular biology are now available to anyone who wants to surf through gene libraries looking for examples of human tissue containing fragments of a desired code. Students interested in subjects like the human genome, gene therapy, or molecular research can now go online and view information in tabular and graphical form. Of course, fifth graders might go after information about genetic engineering on one level, and college students on another. In either case, new media and advancing biomedical technology have to be included in the conversation.

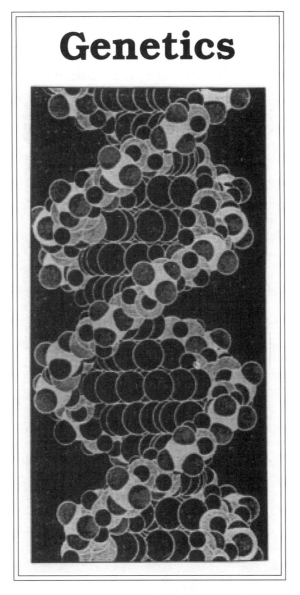

Genetics

Figure 3-2. Genetics

A familiarity with technology is viewed as a proper concern of educational institutions analogous to their concern about language literacy. This makes sense because an important part of any definition of literacy is the ability to communicate in real-world situations. Today that involves gathering information, and experiences and communicating with electronic media. This includes interactive stories in which students become decision-making characters in cinematic narratives.

When high-tech elements are added to the literacy mix, it changes how we view communications and environmental interaction. Multiple technology-based literacies develop and interact with traditional language literacy. Some of the same techniques work for teaching and learning across each medium. Students have long learned to read and write by actually reading, writing, and communicating in supportive situations. In a similar manner, they develop technology-based literacies as they are exposed to authentic experiences that give them a real chance to develop multiple technology-intensive literacy skills.

Whatever the medium, students need to be collectively encouraged to discover ideas, analyze, create, and explore connections. Every time they thoughtfully test their ideas against the outside world they are involved in inquiry. As each person brings his or her unique spirit to the collaborative process, the group takes on enough power to illuminate the consequences of alternative courses of actions. It doesn't diminish the individual personality to say that what matters most is found in our meeting with others.

When it comes to learning, cooperation works better than competition. When learning is done collaboratively, ideas can be shared, and problems and questions become tools for discovery. When we meet and work cooperatively with others, we can accomplish shared goals and get the most out of learning and life. Teachers who use collaborative learning in the classroom have children work in small, mixed-ability groups in which they take responsibility for themselves and for each other. This requires the development of certain social skills. These skills are not innate, they are learned through practice.

Classes new to the collaborative inquiry often assign each member of the group a specific function that is necessary for the successful completion of the group's task. For example: the reader reads the problem, the checker makes sure that it is understood, the animator keeps it interesting and on-task, and the recorder keeps track of the group work and tells the whole class about it. Group achievement depends on how well the group does and how well individuals within the group learn.

Being able to collaboratively deal with some of the clumsy and uncertain aspects of the future is important to understanding, predicting, and applying what is learned in a wide range of situations. Learning with a small circle of friends can help students to navigate around the untidy clutter of doubt and strive for things that had previously exceeded their grasp. Working in community is the best way to gain the confidence and power to see what can be. Table 3-2 lists some digital tools that can be used in collaborative work.

Table 3-2. A Sampling of Collaborative Digital Tools

- E-mail: The most common — and sometimes the most annoying.
- Mailing Lists and Listservs: Good for peer sharing. Limited to a single thread of messages.
- Newsgroups: These work best if the group stays small.
- Web-Conferencing: There are many programs available to make Web pages interactive.
- Multi-User Dungeons or Domains (MUDS) and Object-Oriented MUDS (MOOS): Usually a text-based multi-user simulation environment created by participants to interact for fun, socializing, or even writing software code. Here, users can create "personalities" that stay in the environment even after they leave. Other users can interact with those fictional characters even after their creators are gone and allow an environment to be gradually put together by a succession of participants.
- Virtual Reality Modeling Language (VRML) Chat Systems (Virtual Reality): This language enables you to create three-dimensional multimedia environments or settings that can be viewed using a simple Web browser. No need for the old style helmet and special equipment.

A Combined Sense of Partnership

One of the main reasons that collaborative small-group learning has become so popular is that it motivates and academically engages students within a social setting. It also is a good way for three or four children of mixed backgrounds and capabilities to form friendships as they work toward a common goal. Media can enhance the process, but some face-to-face interaction must take place. Personal responsibility, positive interdependence, interpersonal skill development, and group processing all come into play. In various combinations the group experience can powerfully affect a student's self-esteem and academic achievement.

Collaborative inquiry involves working together to accomplish shared goals that are beneficial to individuals and the group. Students are able to learn together and perform alone, especially in an environment that allows them to actively construct knowledge. In the cooperative classroom, communal responsibility, knowledge construction, and civic engagement are not viewed as optional extras. Everyone is involved, and cooperation becomes part of the fabric of instruction. The collaborative spirit can influence schooling at every level. Building team-based organizational structures in the classroom can also make it easier for teachers to reach out to their peers and ensure that colleagues are successful.

A common element in successful schools is a shared sense of community and a socially integrating sense of purpose. Common interests and common ground make for more civil and intelligent discussions than when all the attention is on individual choice and unconditional rights. As the last few decades have made clear, when there is no limit on individual self-realization, public spaces decay and civic culture is weakened. Schools, like the community in general, need common spaces and educational institutions where people meet and share a life in common.

Organizing for Group Study and Friendship

In organizing groups of two, three, four, or five members it is best to be as heterogeneous as possible. We suggest not going beyond five students in a group. In a difficult class, the teacher can form partnerships by having students list the four people with whom they would most like to work. The teacher then picks the partners with the secret list in hand. (Everyone usually gets at least the number four choice.)

Students need to experience what it's like to work with a mixed group of peers, so it is best to avoid static groups of friends within a classroom. Even a small group can mix children by sex, race, ethnic background, and academic ability. When groups are chosen randomly, students seem to find activities requiring collaboration at least as satisfying and useful as when there is an element of student-teacher choice.

As learning teams discuss a subject, children construct meaning by jointly working on solutions to problems, raising original problems, and exchanging ideas. Group study offers all students many chances to improve speaking and interpersonal skills as they jointly ask questions and share findings. This is particularly important for children who are not assertive or whose second language is English.

As time goes on, students reveal more about themselves and show more willingness to interact and reward each other. As on a successful sports team, the result is usually more lasting cross-cultural friendships and more acceptance of student differences. Students who work together in mixed-ability groups are also more likely to select mixed racial and ethnic acquaintances and friendships. As heterogeneously grouped students cooperate to reach a common goal, they learn to appreciate and respect each other (Barba, 1995).

Studies of group work at the middle school level show that the self-esteem of girls and boys increases through the use of cooperative academic activities and team sports (Cohen, Lotan, & Catanzarite, 1990). Research indicates that the use of cooperative learning groups also improves students' problem-solving abilities. The use of mixed-ability grouping increases students' concept of acquisition and feelings of social confidence in dealing with networking technology (Ramirez & Castanada, 1994). Even those early childhood educators who do not believe in using computers with young children have found the Internet useful for collaborating with colleagues around the world.

Online or off-line, peer tutoring is an effective way of bridging linguistic barriers for bilingual or bicultural students (Watson, 1991). When it is done right, collaborative inquiry experiences address academic and skill needs much better than a steady diet of solitary and isolated learning activities (Barba, 1995).

Getting Teamwork Started in the Classroom

Conceptual knowledge is constructed over time by learners within a meaningful social setting. Students talking and working together on a project or problem experience the fun and experience of sharing ideas and information. When students individually construct knowledge within a social setting, they have opportunities to compare knowledge, talk it over with peers, ask questions, justify their position, confer, and arrive at a consensus. Cooperative interaction with others is an important element in giving all students an opportunity to make sense of what they are learning. It also helps to prepare students for today's society, in which combining energies with others creates a team approach to solving problems that is valued in the world of work, community, and leisure.

The learning climate of the classroom strongly influences such things as self-esteem, motivation, discipline, and expression, as well as individual and group achievement. Getting started with collaborative inquiry means defining student and teacher responsibilities. The percentage of highly qualified teachers is one of the strongest predictors of student achievement (Darling-Hammond, 1999). One of the first steps is usually instructing students in how to work together. The classroom has to be organized so that it is easier for students to develop and practice group process skills. Collaboration will not take place with students sitting in rows facing the teacher. Desks must be pushed together in small groups or replaced with small tables to facilitate group interaction.

Changing the classroom organization so that students are in a supportive environment with face-to-face contact requires changes in the physical structure. This may mean adding work tables or pushing chairs together to form comfortable work spaces that are conducive to open communication. Collaboration will not occur in a classroom that requires students to always raise their hands to speak. Active listening is not sitting quietly as a teacher or another student drones on. It requires spontaneous and polite interruptions where everyone has an equal chance to speak and interact. However, others must be allowed to complete a thought; students cannot just break into the conversation in midsentence. Everyone should get to ask a question or make a comment. It may be best not to make students put their hands up first. Encourage the more talkative class members to let everyone else make a contribution before they make another point.

Collaborative inquiry will involve some change in the noise level of the classroom. Sharing and working together even in controlled environments will be louder than an environment in which students work silently from textbooks. With experience, teachers can learn to keep the noise constructive. A little reasoning (regarding rules) is important for children. Responsible behavior must be developed and encouraged with consistent classroom patterns. Strictly authoritarian approaches to discipline, however, will not work well if we expect students to be responsible for their own learning and behavior.

When collaborative problem-solving is over, students should spend some time reflecting on the group work. What worked well, and how might the process be improved? Students and teachers need to be involved in evaluating learning products and the cooperative group environment.

Effective interpersonal skills are essential not just for a collaborative inquiry activity; they also benefit students in later educational pursuits and when they enter the work force. Social interactions are fundamental to negotiating meaning and building a personal rendition of knowledge. Mixed-ability learning groups have proven effective across the curriculum. It is important to involve students in establishing rules for active group work. Rules should be kept simple and might include the following:

- Everyone is responsible for his or her own work.
- Productive talk is desired.
- Each person is responsible for his or her own behavior.
- Try to learn from others within your small group.
- Everyone must be willing to help anyone who asks.
- Ask the teacher for help if no one in the group can answer the question.

Group roles and individual responsibilities should be clearly defined and arranged so that each group member's contribution is unique and essential. If the learning activities require materials, students may be required to take responsibility for assembling and storing them. Unlike competitive and individualistic goal structures, the operative pronoun in collaborative inquiry is *we*, not *me*. Teamwork and electronic media production are natural partners, as illustrated by the following examples.

1. *Collaborative video publishing.* Before the end of the 1980s, Apple Computer and its software partners gave schools the tools to do desktop publishing. At the beginning of the 21st century, the same group made video publishing as easy as desktop paper publishing. Collaboration often takes place in the print medium, but with video it is a basic requirement. Students can now create sophisticated special effects, animated captions, and sound effects. Small, inexpensive, digital cameras and microphones make for good shots and easy editing. In fact, the video editing software now comes with many of the new Macintosh computers. Our students use a Macintosh DV model, a digital camera, and iMovie software. After they complete their digital creations, they like to put their work on the Web — music videos, short video travelogues, brief news reports, public service announcements, and so on.

2. *Problem solving in collaborative classrooms.* Developing good inquiry skills takes time and practice. Students need ample opportunities for collaborative hands-on learning. This means con-

crete experiences with media tools and actual phenomena. In a classroom that values teamwork, teachers provide time for students to grapple with problems, try out strategies, discuss, experiment, explore, and evaluate.

A key element in collaborative classrooms is group interdependence. This means that the success of each individual depends on the success of each of the other group members. Student investigations, team discussions, and group projects go hand in hand with preparing students for the new information, knowledge, and work arrangements that they will come across throughout life.

Whatever variation of collaborative inquiry a teacher chooses, students can be given opportunities to integrate their learning through interactive discovery experiences and applying their problem-solving skills. Whatever the subject, it is more important to emphasize the reasoning involved in working on a problem than getting "the answer." Near the end of a group project, the teacher can develop more class unity by pointing out how each small-group research effort contributes to the class goal of understanding and exploring a topic. Teachers need to model attitudes and present themselves as collaborative problem solvers and models of inquiry. They do this by letting students know that learning is a lifelong process for teachers and other adults. Teachers should share with students some of their more positive professional development experiences.

A Collaborative Group Problem-Solving Model

As far as our schools are concerned, collaborative problem solving means helping children to understand the forces of nature. As Lev Vygotsky has noted, learning is social.

Planning for Problem Solving

1. The teacher, with input from the students, generates an interesting problem to investigate.

2. The teacher organizes the class for group investigation.

3. The teacher prepares students by explaining cooperative learning and putting some charts up in the room that outline the process and explain roles like reader (reads the problem), checker (makes sure the problem is understood), animator (keeps everyone on task and interested), and recorder (gets all the ideas down for a whole-class report).

(Once students get used to group work you can drop the assign-
ment of roles.)

Problem-Solving Implementation

- The concern, question, or problem to be investigated is
  presented.
- The class brainstorms and determines topics to be
  studied.
- The class organizes into interest-based research teams.
- Individuals within the teams assume their roles and the
  group cooperatively plans its investigation.
- Research teams carry out their inquiry and organize their
  findings.
- The group project is briefly presented to the whole class,
  and all the groups pool information to address the original question or problem.
- Follow-up: The students are held individually accountable for their work. Evaluation may be done with performance assessments, portfolios, projects, experimental
  results, or whatever. Teams are sometimes given group
  rewards based on their individual accomplishments and
  how each group's work contributes to the class understanding of a topic.

Activities and Resources

Phase 1: Brainstorm. Generate ideas in small groups. Make
no negative comments about any of the ideas presented. Encourage unusual ideas and generate as many as possible. Have
a recorder write down every idea presented. Build on other's ideas
whenever possible. (Sometimes the wildest ideas work best, and
sometimes they stay wild.)

Phase 2: Evaluate. Each group's members pick out a few of
their best ideas, and a few of the funniest, to share with the
other groups. Problem example adapted from a version of Daniel
Defoe's *Robinson Crusoe*: "You are cast ashore on a desert island
with nothing but a large leather belt and a large belt buckle.
Brainstorm how you can use what you have to survive — and
possibly get rescued." After 10 or 12 minutes the ban on criticism is over. Pick the four best ideas and the three funniest.
Each group shares with the whole class.

Media experiences from inside and outside the classroom provide access to learning for all students. Adding to and drawing

on a shared media culture as the basis for collaborative inquiry help students to understand and create across technology platforms and disciplines.

Collaborative Homework Help Sites

Children can go online to compare notes with friends, strangers, experts, and digital tutors.

- Homework Central (www.homeworkcentral.com) has a large database of linked sites that will help students of all ages with all kinds of assignments.
- America Online Homework Helper. In general, AOL is a shortcut for students who should be learning how to find the wide range of information on the Web, but AOL's Homework Helper section has really worked for us. It has thousands of volunteer teachers and peer tutors to help with just about anything, and it is divided into sections — from Kids Only to Teens and beyond.
- Infoplease Homework Center (www.kids.infoplease.com/homework/index.html). This site can help students to solve all kinds of homework problems. It has a table of contents on the left side of the screen and a central search box that allows you to search the site's almanacs, encyclopedia, and dictionary. In addition, you can ask an expert specific questions.

There are other good homework sites, like Ask Jeeves for Kids, but these three are our favorites for cooperative group work.

Teaching the Cooperative Group Lesson

It is important that students understand problem and hypothesis formation. As they work together to find a solution, there are some strategies that we have found helpful. During the initial introduction of the lesson, the teacher can help students to understand the problem and establish guidelines for the group's work. The teacher presents or reviews the necessary concepts or skills with the whole class and poses a part of the problem or an example of a problem for the class to try. Opportunities for discussion are provided. The actual group problem is then presented after the conceptual overview. The class is encouraged to discuss and clarify the problem task.

Students then work cooperatively to solve problems. The teacher observes, listens to the groups' ideas, and offers assistance as needed. The teacher is also responsible for providing extension activities when a group finishes early. If a group is having difficulties, the teacher helps it to discover what is known so far, poses a simple example, or perhaps points out a misconception or erroneous idea of the group. Sometimes group members have trouble getting along or focusing on what they are supposed to be doing. At this time it may be necessary to refocus the group's attention by asking questions such as: What are you supposed to be doing? What is the task? How will you get organized? What materials do you need? Who will do what?

After the problem task and group exploration are completed, students again meet as a whole class to summarize and present their findings. Groups present their solutions and share their processes. When the processes are shared, both group procedures and problem-solving strategies are summarized.

Questions might include: How did you organize the task? What problems did you have? What method did you use? Was your group method effective? Did anyone have a different method or strategy for solving the problem? Do you think your solution makes sense? Encourage students to generalize from their results. What other problem does this remind you of? What other follow-up experiments could you try based on your findings? Students are encouraged to listen to and respond to other students' comments. It may also be helpful to make notes of the responses on the chalkboard to help summarize the class data at the close of the lesson.

Integrated Collaborative Inquiry Activities

Learning moves from the social to the personal and back to the social. In the social setting of a collaborative group, students can spot problems while discussing, defining, rejecting, and accepting suggestions. The idea is to help students to develop productive relations with others based on respect, trust, caring, and cooperation. Whether two students are working together or a small group is providing feedback to a writer, the collaborative effort can be invigorating.

For students to successfully complete their collaborative learning tasks, they need to negotiate, compromise, cooperate, and arrive at a synthesis based on rational thought. In collaborative inquiry, students have a better chance to explore ideas, justify their views, and synthesize knowledge within a supportive environment.

One of the key features of collaborative inquiry is that students give and receive help. Group support helps to create a learning environment in which it is safe to make mistakes and to learn from those mistakes. Another structural element in collaboration is maximizing social interaction and focusing on learning that is exciting and pleasurable. Collaborative inquiry does not require adapting one's thinking to the person "in charge." On the contrary, it encourages contributing to a shared understanding of knowledge.

In a collaborative setting the teacher helps children to gain confidence in their own ability and the group's ability to work through problems and consequently to rely less on the teacher as the sole knowledge source. Students are motivated more by the social contact with their peers and by their sense of achievement as they succeed in challenging tasks through the group effort rather than through strict, step-by-step teacher direction.

Bridge Building

Objectives. This is an interdisciplinary science and math activity that reinforces communication skills, group process, social studies, language arts, the arts, mathematics, science, and technology.

Materials. Lots of newspaper, masking tape, one large heavy rock, and one cardboard box. Have students bring in stacks of newspaper, approximately a 1 foot pile of newspapers per small group. Bridges are a tribute to technological efforts that employ community planning, engineering efficiency, mathematical precision, aesthetics, group effort, and construction expertise.

Procedures. For the first part of this activity, divide students into groups of about four. Each group will be responsible for investigating one aspect of bridge building.

Group 1: Research. This group is responsible for going to the library and looking up facts about bridges, collecting pictures of bridges, and bringing back information to be shared with the class.

Group 2: Aesthetics, Art, Literature. This group must discover songs, books, paintings, other artwork, and so forth that deal with bridges.

Group 3: Measurement, Engineering. This group must discover design techniques, blueprints, angles, and measurements of actual bridge designs. If possible, visit a local bridge to look at the structural design. Each group presents its findings to the class. Have the group representatives get together to present their findings to the class. Allow time for questions and discussion.

The second part of this activity involves actual bridge construction with newspapers and masking tape.

1. Assemble the collected stacks of newspaper, the tape, the rock, and the box at the front of the room. Divide the class into groups. Each group is instructed to take a newspaper pile and several rolls of masking tape. Explain that the group will be responsible for building a stand-alone bridge using only the newspapers and tape. The bridge is to be constructed so that it will support the large rock and so that the box can pass underneath.

2. Planning is crucial. Each group is given 10 minutes of planning time in which its members are allowed to talk and plan together. During the planning time they are not allowed to touch the newspapers and tape, but they are encouraged to pick up the rock and make estimates of how high the box is, make a sketch of the bridge, or assign group roles of responsibility.

3. At the end of the planning time, students are given about 15 minutes to build the bridges. During this time there is no talking among the group members. They may not handle the rock or the box — only the newspapers and the tape. (A few more minutes may be necessary to ensure that all groups have a chance of getting their constructions to meet at least one of the two "tests" (the rock or the box). If a group finishes early, it can add some artistic flourishes to its bridge or watch the building process in other groups. (With children you may not want to stop the process until each group can pass at least one "test.")

Evaluation. Stop all groups after the allotted time. Survey the bridges with the class and allow each group to try to pass the two tests for the bridges. Students get to pick which test is done first. Does the bridge support the rock? Does the box fit underneath? Discuss the design of each bridge and how it compares to the bridges researched earlier. Try taking some pictures of the completed works before dismantling them and putting them in a recycling bin. Awards could be given for the most creative bridge design, the most sturdy bridge, the tallest, the widest, the best cooperative group, and so on. Remember that each group will be proud of its bridge.

As an optional follow-up activity, have each group measure its bridge and design a blueprint (including angles, length, and width of the bridge) so that another group could build the bridge by following this model.

Investigate Your Time Line

Objectives. Working in groups of four or five, students make a time line of the ages of the people in their groups and the events in their lives, then compare the events in their lives with those of other students in their group (e.g., "The most important event for me when I was 5 years old was . . ."). The students record and report the results.

Background Information. A time line can show different cultural and ethnic patterns. Students are able to see how maturity affects decisions. A time line exercise is designed to find out how time changes students' math and science perceptions.

Materials. A 13-foot long piece of butcher paper for each group (assuming that no one is older than 12), rulers, fine-point markers, a teacher-prepared time line model to post on the board for the students to use as a model.

Procedures. The teacher explains that the students will be working in cooperative groups to make time lines of the ages and lives of the people in their groups. Students are divided into groups of four or five, and materials are passed out to each group. The teacher explains his or her model time line and gives students the following directions for making their own time lines:

- Find out the ages of the people in the group; who is the oldest, next oldest, youngest, and so on.
- Start the time line on January 1 of the year in which the oldest person in the group was born.
- End the time line on December 31 of the current year.
- Use a different color marker to mark off each year.
- Each year equals 1 foot and each month equals 1 inch. (To do this activity in a college class, use 3 inches for each year instead of 1 foot, and a quarter inch for each month.)
- At the bottom of each year write the important events in students' lives.
- Use a color key with the colors of markers along with each student's name to identify the student. Students can put a dot or a star by the important events in their lives such as birthdays or birth of siblings.

Closure. A volunteer from each group presents the group's time line and posts it on the classroom bulletin board.

An Icy Journey into Scientific Inquiry

Objectives. This activity will introduce the scientific inquiry process in a collaborative setting, enable students to ask questions, make predictions, and find answers through experimentation, and develop observation, communication, and cooperative group skills.

Materials. Balloons, flashlights, magnifying glasses, salt, sugar, food coloring, containers to hold the ice, and 6-inch balls of ice for groups of three or four students.

Introduction. Ask students what they know about ice — either in groups or with the whole class. How does water freeze and melt, and how does ice get used? Students can act like scientists and conduct scientific experiments and try different things with ice as they explore questions their small group finds interesting.

Procedures. Put the piece of ice at the center of each group (use a small table if you can). Encourage students to touch and observe the ice but not pick it up. The first phase is for observation. Ask the students what will happen if someone in their group shines a flashlight beam onto the ice. The idea is to generate some predictions. Use a felt-tip pen to put them on a large sheet of paper or put them on the chalkboard. The next step is to give each group a flashlight and have students take turns experimenting. Have them record what they observe and decide how to communicate it.

The same procedure can be followed with salt, sugar, and food coloring—making predictions, doing experiments, and observing what they discover. The groups may rotate so that students get to see the differences in texture, color, clarity, and so on. Each table should end up at the original ice ball and do a final drawing based on careful observation.

Evaluation. Encourage students to relate and apply the information they learn from the ice ball activity to scientific inquiry. This includes making predictions, observations, and working collaboratively. (We acknowledge San Francisco teacher Sarah Peterson for this activity.)

Ranking Skills Desired by
Fortune 500 Companies

Mix up the order of the 13 most important skills that Fortune 500 companies are looking for in employees. Be sure to point out that this is a composite ranking and that companies vary somewhat in terms of priorities. Another point to make is that nearly everyone involved is a college graduate, and it is assumed that everyone can read, write, and compute.

The correct order:

1. Teamwork
2. Problem solving
3. Interpersonal skills
4. Oral communication
5. Listening
6. Personal career development
7. Creative thinking
8. Leadership
9. Goal-setting motivation
10. Writing
11. Organizational effectiveness
12. Computation
13. Reading

Students can work in groups of three or four to come up with their ranking. Compare to the correct answers, figure the difference with the group answer, and add up the differences on each of the 13 points.

Multicultural Awareness Activity

Objectives. This activity is designed to make middle school students aware of multicultural differences in values and approaches to very fundamental societal practices, and to teach them to be sensitive to the feelings and thoughts of their classmates who may either come from other countries or have family members in other countries.

Introduction. Organize participating students so that there is equal or nearly equal representation of students of different racial, ethnic, or national backgrounds in each team of four. For instance, make sure that each group has one Chinese, one Latino, one German, and one Native American student (They may be either foreign-born or U.S.-born). It is important to find out where they were raised for the most part during their early years. Of course, many students represent mixed nationalities. Ask them which one they identify with the most and whose values they think they have practiced the most.

Procedures. First of all, make sure that there are about four members in each group and that each group has a mixture of nationalities. Have the group elect a leader. Ask the different groups to write down their responses to the following questions. Give the students a day or two to research the answers and the time to fill out the form below.

1. What does "time" mean in your culture? Have you been taught by your family or friends to move fast and get things done on time? Or have you been taught to pay more attention to the people you're dealing with and make the work "wait"? Have you been told that "time is money" and therefore "don't waste it," or that there's always "lots of time" and so "don't hurry, but live life well"?

2. What have your parents taught you about "following your dreams"? Did they tell you to do what you love or whatever it is that you want to do, or did they encourage you to do what is honorable and acceptable to your family, relatives, or society?

3. What have you been taught about making friends? What is most important in making friends?

4. What about gift giving? What were you taught about when it is appropriate to give gifts? To whom? For what reasons? What kinds of gifts should you give them?

5. What have you been taught about the importance of family and your relatives?

Ask students who were born and raised in the United States to interview their parents, other family members, and friends about the answers to these questions. Have the students recall what was taught to them at home and (if relevant) in schools they attended in their countries of origin. The important thing is to help students reconstruct the value system of the cultures they identify with the most. Then have the students fill out the following form:

Values I Have Been Taught
1. What I think of these values (e.g., I believe in these values, or
    I don't think they are useful to me today.)
2. What am I actually doing today with respect to these values?
    *   Value of "time"
    *   "Dream work" and success in life
    *   Friendships
    *   Gift giving
    *   Family and relatives

When the students return with their answers, go around the
room and have each student share the information. Then have a
second round of discussions; this time, ask each student how he
or she would like to be treated by other classmates who believe
in different values: "Now that you know what the values in your
culture are, how would you like your classmates from other cultures to treat you to show a better understanding of your culture?" (Teachers should not yet inject ideas on how to respect
others' unique cultural values. That will be done at the conclusion of the exercise. Right now, just listen to the students' own
ideas about what they think constitutes "feeling safe" in a
multicultural classroom setting.)

It is possible that students of other national origins have as-
similated into North American culture and are not experiencing
"cultural clash" or "culture shock" because they were born and
raised in the United States. It is still instructive to know what
they may have been taught and to highlight the differences between those values and what they are actually putting into practice in their daily lives. Students who have successfully
acculturated in the United States can share some ideas about
how they reconciled any conflicts in values between the two (or
more) cultures.

End the exercise with a brief lecture on guidelines in dealing
with multicultural social settings. Teachers should conduct their
own research on safe cross-cultural tips to follow that encourage
mutual respect and intercultural sensitivity among students.
Suggest such things as the following:
1. Do not jump to conclusions or premature judgments when
    you're dealing with classmates from other countries. They
    may interpret the situation differently.
2. Just because some classmates—especially those from
    Asia—are quiet in class does not mean that they lack in-
    telligence. Most of the time, they are thinking about what
    is being discussed in class. They are quiet because they

have been taught to wait for someone in authority, such as a teacher, to start and lead the discussion.

3. Try to talk some more with your classmates, especially those who were born and raised in other countries. Try to find out what they were taught as children about different things—what it means to do well in school, to respect parents, or to be successful in life.

(Thanks to Dr. Rebecca Angeles, Computer Information Systems Department, Bentley College, for this exercise.)

Changing Attitudes About Collaboration and Learning

Some students may require a shift in values and attitudes if a collaborative learning environment is to succeed. The traditional school experience has taught many students that the teacher is there to validate their thinking and direct learning. Getting over years of learned helplessness may take time.

Attitudes change as students learn to work cooperatively. As they share rather than compete for recognition, many children find time for reflection and assessment. Small groups can write collective stories, edit each other's writing, solve problems, correct homework, prepare for tests, investigate questions, examine artifacts, work on a computer simulation, brainstorm an invention, create a sculpture, or arrange music. Working together is also a good way for students to synthesize what they have learned, collaboratively present to a small group, coauthor a written summary, or communicate concepts.

It is important that students understand that simply "telling an answer" or "doing someone's work" is not helping a classmate to learn. Helping involves learning to ask the right question so that someone can grasp the meaning, or explaining with an example. These understandings must be actively and clearly explained, demonstrated, and developed by the teacher.

A major benefit of collaborative inquiry is that students are provided with group stimulation and support. The small group provides safe opportunities for trial and error as well as a safe environment for asking questions or expressing opinions. More students get chances to respond, raise ideas, or ask questions. As each student brings unique strengths and experiences to the group and contributes to the group process, respect for individual differences is enhanced.

The group also acts as a motivator. We all feel a little nudge when others are involved. Many times ideas are pushed beyond what an individual would attempt or suggest. The quality and quantity of thinking increases as more ideas are added, surpassing what the individual could do alone. Group interaction enhances idea development, and students have many opportunities to be teachers as well as learners. Simultaneously, the small group structure extends children's resources as they are encouraged to pool strategies and share information. More withdrawn students become more active. Students who often have a hard time sticking to a task receive group assistance so they can learn to monitor their time better and become productive members of the group. Students soon learn that they are capable of validating their own values and ideas. This frees teachers to move about, work with small groups, and interact in a more personal manner with students.

Reciprocal Teaching

Reciprocal teaching recognizes that learning is a social process in which explanations from someone more knowledgeable can be internalized and become part of an individual's thinking process. The basic idea is to have a teacher and students, or just students in a group, discuss a concept and help individuals within the group to construct meaning. Comprehension is still an individual task, but group interaction, support, and the exchange of ideas all contribute to changing understandings and perspectives. Collaborative group discussion and teamwork can deepen understanding and broaden the perspectives of everyone involved.

An example of reciprocal teaching would be to have everyone in the group read a passage and take turns leading the discussion. Question generating, predicting, clarifying, and summarizing are all part of the process. To generate questions, students must seek out information that can provide a basis for well-formed questions. Before reading a section of text or using the Internet, students can make predictions based on prior knowledge, illustrations, charts, an introductory paragraph, or subheadings. An example of clarifying would be having students note words, concepts, and other things that might get in the way of comprehension. Summarizing may be thought of as paraphrasing and highlighting major concepts. It can also be a springboard for making predictions about the content of the next chapter or subject matter concept.

Getting Started With Reciprocal Teaching

Make sure that students understand that it is good to help each other. Give students an idea of how to be like the teacher in a small group. For instance, ask them, "Have you ever wanted to switch places with the teacher?" Tell them that at the end they will evaluate group effectiveness. Explain question generating, prediction, clarifying, and summarizing.

To fully comprehend what they are studying, students must learn to ask themselves questions about content. Reciprocal teaching is a good way to make that happen. As the class begins to use this approach, the teacher's role is to stimulate thinking with good questions. Inferential, critical, and creative thinking has to be modeled, but once the students have figured out how the teacher designs good questions they can begin to do it themselves.Teachers and students take turns leading discussions about the meaning of concepts that are being covered. Reciprocal questioning, predicting, clarifying issues, and summarizing fosters understanding and helps students to take on more responsibility for developing powerful ideas and for each other.

Sometimes we have students write down questions and ask their peers to come up with the answers. As they prove themselves, more and more responsibility is placed on the students. Of course, from time to time the teachers must still model higher level questioning techniques that can lead to more effective collaborative inquiry. Students quickly learn to stop at designated places in a text to share thinking and elicit responses to particular types of inquiries.

Reciprocal teaching is a highly effective approach for generating back-and-forth, student-to-student and student-to-teacher dialogue. Whatever their age, students can learn to act as apprentices who gradually assume more and more teaching responsibility for partners or small groups. As a collaborative inquiry procedure, reciprocal teaching has produced positive results across grade levels and subject matter.

Skillful Collaboration Enhances the Curriculum

Collaborative inquiry has proven itself as an effective way to bring about change in a traditional school environment. Collaborative activities, group problem solving, reciprocal teaching, and cross-age tutoring are now generally accepted as useful tools to help students get the most out of any subject. By collaboratively exploring new concepts in different contexts, students can internalize mental images, perform actions, and discover underlying concepts. It works best when students do the following:

- Perceive the need for depending on each other

- Learn how to work well in a small group
- Feel responsibility towards other group members
- Provide each other with specific feedback
- Hold both the group and themselves accountable

To gain and share expertise, team members challenge each other's thinking in a way that doesn't breed conformity or hostility. Work teams can also be used to provide students with a support network that can gradually be withdrawn as children move to higher levels of confidence. In collaborative inquiry, mutual achievement and caring for one another can result in learning actually becoming more personalized. Students and teachers can come to view each other as a learning community of collaborators who help group members with cognitive, emotional, physical, and social change.

Collaborative inquiry requires a set of strategies to encourage having students cooperate while learning in a variety of settings and disciplines. The process involves promoting positive interdependence by dividing the workload, providing joint rewards, holding individuals accountable, and getting students actively involved in helping each other to master the topic being studied. Creative social engagement is paramount. This approach to active team learning is more than an innovation in itself; it is a catalyst for other changes in curriculum, instruction, and schooling. Students and teachers are viewed as being rooted in a network of familial and community relationships that make up a civil society. Like an extended family, everyone cares about individual and mutual achievement. Individual rights are balanced by reciprocal obligation and mutual interdependence.

Collaborative inquiry can be used with confidence across subjects and grade levels to explore meaning and to help students take responsibility for each other. The process includes gradually internalizing instructional concepts through interactions with peers and adults. Individual and group reflection are encouraged along the way. By building on group energy and idealism, the thinking, learning, and doing process can be pushed forward in any medium (Figure 3-3).

GET THERE ANY WAY YOU CAN

Creating the Inclusive / Cooperative Classroom

Figure 3-3. Creating the Inclusive/Cooperative Classroom

A Shared Journey
Into a New Century

By tapping into students' natural curiosity, collaborative inquiry can go a long way toward helping schools to achieve academic and social goals. It is a disciplined and imaginative way of thinking, exploring, and coming together in community with others. Becoming a contributing member of a learning team can help students by promoting self-discovery, higher level reasoning, and social cohesion. Putting these human factors first is key to using technology effectively.

In collaborative inquiry, student questions can be fashioned in a way that connects the big ideas that cut across disciplines.

As they work in pairs or in small, mixed-ability groups, students can take more responsibility for helping themselves and others to learn. More and more teachers are using active team learning to enrich their lessons and get around some of the more solitary aspects of educational technology. As teachers learn when and how to structure instruction cooperatively, the process transforms itself from a hot new method into a routine part of the day-to-day instructional program.

We now have the technological elements necessary for interactive access to a personalized set of social learning experiences. Literacy and culture around the world are increasingly filtered through technology.

From television and film to the Internet and electronic games, the deliberate creation of unreality is shaping our perception of the world. It is little wonder that schools in the developed world are looking to media education to help students to develop the intellectual tools required to sort out what is fantasy from what is real. As schools are being pushed to integrate electronic media into the classroom, we would do well to remember that the key to success is making sure that the curriculum drives the technology and not vice versa.

The various transformations that society is experiencing at the beginning of the 21st century are the result of new ideas, technologies, globalization, and the emergence of new mindsets. In the more developed countries, education and related technologies are beginning to reflect constructivist theories of learning; schools are being urged to spend less time transmitting information and more time supporting students' efforts to construct their own understanding.

The habits of the mind and the emotions of the heart associated with technology and collaborative inquiry can be like a breath of fresh air. They interject a communal element into our increasingly isolated and fragmented existence. There is little wonder that, in one guise or another, collaborative group work has become one of the most widely used instructional innovations. Computers and their technological associates are hot on its heels. When various combinations of these two powerful forces come together, they are bound to make a lasting impact on curriculum and instruction. To have a positive influence on education, the information and communication technologies being created must attend to the social nature of human learning. By helping us to meet and collaborate with other people, technological tools can help us to accomplish shared goals and get the most out of learning and life.

References

Angeles, R. (2000). *Multicultural inquiry for mutual collaborative understanding.* Unpublished Manuscript, Bentley College, Waltham, MA.

Barba, R. (1995). *Science in the multicultural classroom.* Needham Heights, MA: Allyn & Bacon.

Braine, G. (1998). Teaching writing on local area networks. In C. S. Ward & W. A. Renandya (Eds.), *Computers and language learning* (pp. 63–76). Singapore: SEAMEO Regional Language Centre.

Burns, A. (1999). *Collaborative action research for English language teachers.* Cambridge: Cambridge University Press.

Clandinin, D. J. & Connelly, F. M. (2000). *Narrative inquiry: Experience and story in quantitive research.* San Francisco: Jossey-Bass.

Clarke, J., Weidman, R., & Eadie, S. (1990). *Together we learn.* Toronto: Prentice-Hall.

Cohen, E. G. (1994). Restructuring the classroom: Conditions for productive small groups. *Review of Educational Research* vol. 64, pp. 1–35.

Cohen, E. G., Lotan, R., & Catanzarite, L. (1990). Treating status problems in the cooperative classroom. In S. Sharan (Ed.), *Cooperative learning: Theory and research* (pp. 203–229). New York: Praeger.

Darling-Hammond, L. (1999). *Teacher quality and student achievement.* Palo Alto, CA: Center for the Study of Teaching and Learning.

Davidson, N. (Ed.). (1990). *Cooperative learning in mathematics.* Menlo Park, CA: Addison-Wesley.

Dixon-Krauss, L. (1996). *Vygotsky in the classroom: Mediated literacy instruction and assessment.* White Plains, NY: Longman.

Gardner, H. (1999). *Intelligence reframed: Multiple intelligences for the 21st century.* New York: Basic Books.

Hannaford, C. (1995). *Smart moves.* Arlington, VA: Great Ocean.

Heinich, R., Molenda, M., Russell, J., & Smaldino, S. (1999). *Educational media and technologies for learning.* Columbus, OH: Merrill/Prentice-Hall.

Lazear, D. G. (1999). *Eight ways of knowing: Teaching for multiple intelligences: A handbook of techniques for expanding intelligence.* Arlington Heights, IL: SkyLight Training.

Lee, C., Ng, M., & Jacobs, G. M. (1998). Cooperative learning in the thinking classroom. In M. L. Quah & W. K. Ho (Eds.), *Thinking processes: Going beyond the surface curriculum* (pp. 223–237). Singapore: Simon & Schuster.

Ramirez, M., & Castanada, A. (1994). *Cognitive strategy research: Educational applications*. New York: Springer-Verlag.

Slavin, R. E. (1990). *Cooperative learning: Theory, research, and practice*. Englewood Cliffs, NJ: Prentice-Hall.

Slavin, R. E. (1995). *Cooperative learning: Theory,research and practice* (2nd ed.). Boston: Allyn & Bacon.

Slavin, R. E. (2000). *Educational psychology: Theory and practice*. Boston: Allyn & Bacon.

Snodgrass, D. M. (2000). *Collaborative learning in middle and secondary schools: Applications and assessments*. Larchmont, NY: Eye On Education 2000.

Sprenger, M. (1999). *Learning & memory: The brain in action.* Alexandria, VA: Association for Supervision and Curriculum Development.

Stasson, M. F., Kameda, T., Parks, C. D., Zimmerman, S. K., & David, J. H. (1991). Effects of assigned group consensus requirement on group problem solving and group members' learning. *Social Psychology 54* (1), 25–35.

Watson, S. B. (1991). Cooperative learning and group educational modules: Effects on cognitive achievements. *Journal of Research in Science Teaching 28* (2), 141–146.

4. Process Skills Across the Curriculum: Engaging Students With Interdisciplinary Themes

The greatest discoveries have always been those that forced us to rethink our beliefs about the universe and our place in it. As we comprehend the scale of the universe, we must also be filled with wonder that fragile, self replicating specks of matter trapped on a tiny planet could have managed to figure this all out.

—Robert L. Park

For decades the processes of science have been recognized as the foundation for scientific activity. Process skills are the associated intellectual tools for understanding the natural world. These skills and understandings can serve as a solid base for inviting student inquiry into the big ideas that link several areas of knowledge. As tools of science, technology and mathematics have always been valued partners in centering learning on the deep themes that underlie content. They can help students to make connections between concepts as they strive to understand interdisciplinary themes.

The process of doing science is just as important as learning about science. Process-oriented lessons go beyond teaching facts and theories to making sure that children learn to do science by using some of the same methods and technologies as actual scientists. As children learn science by doing science, they learn to ask their own questions about things that interest them, and they learn to combine new experiences with information they already possess. This is the essence of constructivism: building knowledge from personal experience and thought. Technology can help by providing aspects of the world that cannot be experienced directly. Beyond this, the ability to critically and creatively process and use information and communication technology is an important component of any definition of literacy, including the scientific variety.

Many process skills are acquired through a questioning process and can direct the searcher to knowledge and new ideas. Along the way students also learn to raise new questions and new possibilities for examination. An ever enlarging pattern of integrated understandings leads to the construction of deeper and more meaningful knowledge. It is little wonder that related methods of active learning, scientific reasoning, and collaborative inquiry are increasingly being used in ways that empower individuals to think and act across the boundaries of academic disciplines.

The Process Approach to Teaching and Learning

> Knowing is not enough; we must apply.
> Willing is not enough; we must do.
> —Goethe

A stone skips across a pond, forming ripples. Thoughts within ideas, images, and conceptions spread out like ripples stretching out to unknown shores. An idea is ignited, questions arise, and the process of discovery begins.

Observing, comparing, classifying, sequencing, problem solving and communicating are all part of what makes process skills important investigative tools. A thorough knowledge of these skills can positively influence how an individual works, thinks, and solves a wide range of problems. A problem often has scientific and technological dimensions. As the science standards point out, "The central distinguishing characteristic between science and technology is the goal: The goal of science is to understand the natural world, and the goal of technology is to make modifications in the world to meet human needs" (National Academy Press, 1996).

Whatever the problem, subject, or issue, students should be invited to use some of the same thinking processes and technological tools that are used by scholars who are searching for new knowledge in their field of study. By using some of the same process tools as those more advanced in the field, students can generate better questions, find out about the world, and apply content to daily life. Thus, the skills learned in one context can form a foundation of understanding that can reach across the core curriculum.

By building a body of knowledge, attitudes, and skills, children build a foundation for future discoveries. Being able to use the knowledge and process skills in a meaningful way is probably the most important objective for students in their learning process. Meaningful learning implies active student control over the content learned as well as being able to practically use the knowledge in a personal way. The curiosity of children must go hand in hand with curriculum content. Manipulating, adapting ideas, learning through experience, creating knowledge, and increasing appreciation for the laws and principles that guide learners can all be enhanced by highly developed process skills (Table 4-1).

As learners construct knowledge (or process, as Jean Piaget explains it) rather than accumulate it, they make the content relevant and personal. Teachers should introduce and help to plan class investigations so that children develop and apply process skills across the curriculum. The understanding of concepts and facts associated with inquiry learning requires practice in one or more of the process skills.

Table 4-1. Key Process Skills

Discovering	Communicating	Exploring
observing	valuing	predicting
inferring	gathering and	estimating
classifying	recording data	experimenting
measuring	graphing	
comparing	using language	
sequencing	sharing with others	
forming relationships		

The Discovering Processes

Discovering examines how students connect and interact with their world; how they make sense or bring order to things around them. It implies direct contacts and manipulation of those contacts into recognizable patterns and structures for interpreting new information. Discovering is based on children's natural curiosity about their environment. Constructivists contend that learners build personal senses of reality as a result of their life experiences. Children have a natural need to know about how things work and survive or how they are unique. The process skills that support discovery learning processes are discussed below.

Observing

Most people tend to associate observation exclusively with the sense of sight, most likely because 80% to 85% of human observations involve sight. To define observation in this way is extremely limiting, however. Effective observation involves all the primary senses working together to gather as much information as possible. It is an immediate reaction to one's environment. Students should be directed to describe what they see, hear, smell, touch, and perhaps taste. Encourage students to try to give some specific measurements to their observations. Teachers should not influence students' observations by adding their own interpretations. Even young children should be able to make good observations. Observations are the foundations for all other inquiry process skills (Figure 4-1). They are the uninterpreted "facts" of science, mathematics, the sounds and symbolisms of words, and the expression of ideas in the literary arts.

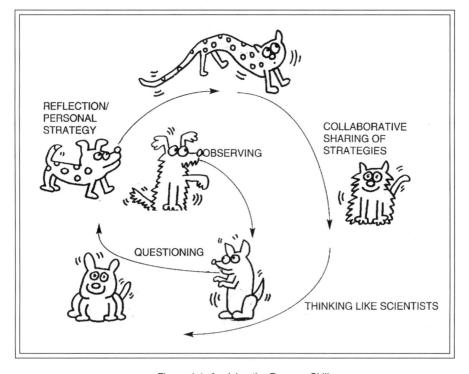

Figure 4-1. Applying the Process Skills

Inferring

Children often make inferences about their observations. Observations and inferences are directly related. Inferences are based on observations and experiences (if the observations are inaccurate or flawed, the inferences will reflect this). Students are often very creative in making inferences based on what they have observed. Inferences extend observation by allowing learners to explain their findings and predict what they think will happen. Are these inferences correct? Inferences either relate to the observations in a logical way and are therefore reasonable, or they don't (Neuman, 1993). The interesting and challenging thing about making inferences is the language that takes place among the students. Language is a powerful tool for gathering and sharing information. Children should therefore be encouraged to talk to each other, the teacher, and other adults while they are engaged in observing and making inferences based on their senses and experiences.

Classifying

Classification is an important part of our lives. Shopping at the supermarket, finding a book in the library, or even setting the dinner table would be a tremendously time-consuming chore if things weren't classified. At a young age children are able to classify or sort objects into groups by color, size, or shape, to rearrange the set, and to put the groups in some kind of order. Writers use classifying skills when they write a story by developing a persona from bits of character traits. In language arts, information can be organized, classified, and categorized when the book that the teacher is reading aloud contains many comparisons or pieces of information.

Measuring

Scientists and mathematicians are constantly measuring. Measuring supplies the hard data necessary to confirm hypotheses and make predictions. It provides firsthand information. Measuring includes gathering data on size, weight, and quantity. Measurement tools and skills have a variety of uses in everyday adult life. Being able to measure connects science and mathematics to the environment. Measurement tools—rulers, thermometers, scales, and so forth—give children opportunities for interdisciplinary learning in subjects such as language arts, social studies, technology, art, and music.

Comparing

Once children learn to observe and describe objects, they soon begin to compare two or more objects. Young children may say that they want more or fewer, and they can tell you what is the same or different. Being able to compare individual as well as sets of objects will help children to decide whether four is more or less than six. Comparing is not just a skill for students in the early grades. Good learning involves comparing other studies, experiments, and conclusions.

Sequencing

Children live with sequences and patterns. They may notice patterns in nature—the symmetry of a leaf, the wings of an insect, or patterns in the classroom—or the tessellations of the floor or ceiling tiles. Sequencing is finding or bringing order to their observations. These interesting patterns all around are enlivened when teachers direct student observation and pattern finding. Literary artists develop their characters from the interactions of human traits and form their stories by articulating the associations among unrelated happenings. The search for patterns take different routes for a painter, a composer, a playwright, or an actor. All must solve their special problems by organizing their ideas.

Forming Relationships

As children compare, classify, and sequence objects, they soon look at the relationships among the objects. Relationships are rules or agreements used to associate one or more objects or concepts with another. Many subjects reflect a collection of relationships among objects or concepts. For example, a concept in nature is that animals have certain needs: air, food, water, and space. A variety of factors affects the ability of wildlife to maintain its survival over time. The most fundamental of life's necessities are the needs mentioned above. Everything in natural systems is interrelated. If one of these needs were eliminated, the animal population would dwindle and die.

Children must create the relationships within and between subjects for themselves. It is critical that we get students to be active mentally, to reflect on things presented in class. That is the way that the mind can construct a relationship (Van de Walle, 1997).

The Communicating Processes

Communication stresses the importance of being able to talk about, write about, describe, and explain a variety of ideas. Symbolism, along with visual aids such as charts and graphs, should become a way of expressing ideas to others. This means that students should learn not only to interpret a subject but also to use the language of that subject within and beyond the classroom. All students gain by regularly talking, writing, drawing, graphing, and using symbols, numbers, and tables to help them think and communicate their ideas. By making sense to others, they indirectly convey the concept in a meaningful way for themselves.

We need to get rid of the idea that what we do in school is somehow removed from everyday experience. Communication is most effective when students express themselves for a real purpose and a real audience.

The process (learning) skills that support the goal of communicating are discussed below in more detail.

Valuing

"Why do I need to know this?" This question is heard frequently by teachers. Valuing emphasizes children's feelings, emotions, and attitudes as they learn various disciplines. From decades of research we have learned that a student's success in a curricular area is often determined by how well his or her personal needs are met in that area. In the meantime, computation for the sake of computation is definitely open to criticism. But reasoning and problem-solving patterns are intimately connected with the very fabric of our society. Employees are searching for solutions to problems that have never been encountered before. Children need to see themselves learning not only skills, but also reasoning and solving problems. Connecting realistic life situations will reinforce the conclusion that this is important.

Helping students to actively apply process skills to a subject requires a different role for the teacher. By guiding and encouraging students to form their own decisions and initiate their own discoveries, the teacher acts more as a mentor or facilitator. Teachers provide many different opportunities for individuals to open new paths, form new discoveries, and direct their own learning. The importance of a value-based curriculum is that students and teachers work together on the subject-matter content. The contributions and personality dynamics of each child are recognized. When content and learning skills are al-

lowed to overlap and reinforce one another, the resulting synergy amplifies learning.

Gathering and Recording Data

The skills of data gathering, analyzing, and recording as well
as using tables and reading graphs provide many opportunities
for representing, interpreting, and recording that apply to every
subject.

Many decisions are based on market research and sales pro-
jections. If these data are to be understood and used, all people
should be able to process such information efficiently. For example, consider the following concepts:

- weather reports (decimals, percentages, probabilities, observing weather patterns, classifying climate zones, identifying weather fronts)
- public opinion polls (sampling techniques and errors of
measurement)
- advertising claims (hypothesis testing)
- monthly government reports involving unemployment, in-
flation, and energy supplies (percentages, prediction, and
extrapolation)

All the media depend on techniques for summarizing information. Radio, television, and newspapers bombard us with sta-
tistical information. The current demand for information
-processing skills continues to grow.

Graphing

Graphing skills include constructing and reading graphs as
well as interpreting graphical information. They should be introduced in the early grades. The data should depend on children's
interest and maturity. Here are a few kinds of survey data that
could be collected in the classroom:

- physical characteristics (height, eye color, shoe size)
- sociological characteristics (birthdays, number in family)
- personal preferences (favorite television shows, favorite
books, favorite sports, favorite food).

Each of these concepts gives students the opportunity to collect data themselves.

Graphs are an important form of communication in science,
mathematics, literature, and social studies. Graphic messages
can provide large amounts of information at a glance. Often graphs
are used to make predictions. There are two rules to remember
about graphing:

1. There are two types of variables on a graph. A manipulated variable, or independent variable, is always plotted along the horizontal axis. The variable that is plotted along the vertical axis is described as the responding variable, or dependent variable. Normally, when the term *manipulated variable* is used, it describes the data that is controlled by the experimenters. After the experimenters gather their data through a survey, they organize it and graph the results.

2. It's important to make the graph large and clear enough for the reader to make interpretations, predictions, or analyses.

Using Language

Language is a window into students' thinking and understanding. For most individuals, oral language is the primary means of communication. One of the overriding objectives in the classroom is to facilitate the use of oral language and listening as a means of communication and learning. Listening to students' language is a valuable way to get feedback about students' efforts. There are many ways to give students opportunities to practise and use language effectively. Effective communication will, of course, depend on topical knowledge as well as on students' being aware of how to go about communicating orally. Self-awareness also fits in—how well one applies oral communication skills. There are many different ways to involve students actively in this process. A few are mentioned here: storytelling, directed reading activities, art (clay modeling, drawing, sculpture), music (playing, singing, listening), oral presentations, small-group discussions, and creative dramatics.

Sharing With Others

The process of sharing helps students to feel more comfortable and less inhibited in speaking before an audience. Sharing their work and ideas allows students the opportunity to develop independence. Again, self-confidence is very important. Whole-class discussions are held after the children have had time to explore a particular activity or idea. Teachers use these group sharing times to summarize and interpret data from explorations. Group sharing is a time for students to discuss their ideas, focus on science and mathematical relationships, and help children to make connections among activities.

Students often find the curriculum most appealing when it helps them to focus on themselves. Young people are in the process of discovering who and what they are. It is necessary for adolescents to form some positive impressions of themselves based on sound observations and evidence.

Figure 4-2. Child Fleeing School
(computer generated image including elements of a painting by Steve Gianakos)

The Exploring Processes

To explore is to examine carefully, to travel in little-known regions for discovery. Exploring means allowing students to reach their own conclusions and decisions. Not only do children have the ability to reach out into their world through self-initiated processes, but they must also be given the opportunity to do so. For teachers, the goal of exploring suggests that students should be provided with many opportunities to direct their own learning. The inquiry processes used in exploring are discussed below in greater detail.

Predicting

Will it snow tomorrow? How long will I remain in San Francisco? Is my car going to last through the semester? These questions can be answered, but only by a guess, not a prediction. They require speculation. How can we turn speculation (a guess) into a prediction? For example, the answer to the question about will it snow tomorrow can be highly speculative, but observers can turn that speculation into a prediction. First, students must know something about current weather conditions. How fast are weather systems moving? From what direction are they moving? What is the temperature, relative humidity, dew point? What kinds of clouds are there? Perhaps it snowed last year at this time. Are there any low pressure systems nearby? What about cold or warm fronts? With this data readily available, students can check past weather conditions. In the past, when conditions were similar, it snowed 50% of the time, so there is a 50-50 chance that it will snow tomorrow, too. Predictions tell us that, given these conditions, it has snowed every time, sometimes, or perhaps never.

Children learn that not all predictions are accurate. Often there is a high degree of uncertainty in predicting. The ability to make predictions is based on skillful observation, inference, quantification, and communication. Students who understand predicting are aware that unforeseen events can change the conditions of a prediction—that 100% accuracy is most unlikely.

Estimating

The curriculum should include estimation so that students can explore estimation strategies, recognize when an estimation is appropriate, determine the reasonableness of the results, and apply estimation in working with quantities, measurement, computation, and problem solving.

Not too many years ago, to compute meant almost exclusively one thing: pencil and paper computation. Today there are many more options; computation by hand is usually a last resort.

First look at the data. Does it require an exact answer, or will an approximate answer do? If an approximate answer will suffice, an estimate can usually be arrived at mentally.

If an exact answer is required, we frequently try to work the computation out in our minds (mental computation). Mental computation is still a more realistic option, but, depending on the numbers involved, a person may have to use other options: a calculator, a computer, or working the problem out by hand. A calculator is almost always the choice, unless there are many similar computations. When computations are related to formulas, then a computer is useful.

If mental computation were always possible or just as fast as making an estimate, there would be little need for estimation skills. Estimation's goal is to quickly determine a result that is adequately accurate for the situation. In everyday life, estimation skills have proven to be tremendously valuable and time-saving. Teaching these skills to students has become more important in recent years.

Experimenting

The basic process skills just discussed are global in their application. For example, students might use the process of inferring to try to understand why their teacher was angry with them in the lab yesterday. A student might sort and classify supplies for the field trip tomorrow. The experimental processes that are described in this section are more limited in their scope and application.

Inquiry processes such as forming a hypothesis, identifying and controlling variables, or analyzing data are skills that are used in a controlled experiment. Hypotheses (a) are not merely educated guesses, (b) are testable, and (c) state a relationship between two variables: a manipulated, or independent, variable and a responding, or dependent, variable. An intervening variable is any other factor that influences the relationship between the independent and dependent variables.

Activities Using Process Skills

Experimenting With Paper Airplanes

Description. Teachers can turn a common classroom distraction into a project of design and discovery. In this activity students will discover that there's more to a paper airplane than just folding and tossing paper. As they work on perfecting design plans, they will learn to hypothesize, experiment, and draw conclusions. Students will work in small groups to design a paper airplane of any size using any or all of the materials provided. Their challenge: to design a plane that will fly farther and straighter than the planes built by the other groups. The exploring process skills of predicting, estimating, and experimenting are applied.

Materials. Seven grades of paper: typing, onion-skin, computer, construction, paper towels, cardboard, milk cartons; paper clips of various sizes; staples; tape; directions for designing paper airplanes.

Objectives. Students will (a) design a plan for their airplane; (b) formulate a hypothesis describing their design and their projection of a successful flight pattern; (c) experiment with the materials and modify or alter their design; (d) identify the variables that influenced the outcome of their investigation and record their efforts; (e) carry out the investigation and generate data; (f) communicate their data through written procedures; and (g) actively participate in a plane-throwing contest.

Procedures

1. Give each group a copy of the paper airplane directions and at least three sheets of paper.

2. Introduce the class to some factors that can affect the performance of paper airplanes. Folding: Symmetry and sharp folds are crucial in designing the plane. Adding weight: A paper airplane needs weight at the front tip (nose). In many cases the folded paper provides the weight, but if the nose isn't heavy enough, the plane will rise up in front, then fall straight down. Paper clips, staples, tape, or additional folds can add weight. If a plane is too heavy it will dive to the ground. To give it more lift, cut and fold flaps on the backs of the wings. If the flaps are folded at 90-degree angles, the plane will fly differently than if the flaps are only slightly turned up.

3. Encourage students to experiment as they adjust the variables. They will learn a lot about trial and error as well as making and testing hypotheses.

4. Groups should test their designs and try out their model experiment. Allow sufficient time for practice.

5. Before the contest begins, the class may wish to design posters (stating their purpose and the skills involved) and invite other classes to watch their science and math airplane contest.

6. As a class, conduct the airplane contest. Airplanes will be judged on how far they fly and how long they stay in the air (use a stopwatch). If students create designs that loop in flight, students may also want to judge the number of circles. The best place to hold the contest is in the school auditorium (no wind, plenty of space). Allow each group to fly its model two or three times, then take the best score.

7. Groups should present their models explaining their hypotheses and assembly method.

Evaluation. Students will have the opportunity to ask questions and share designs and launching tips with their classmates. Students should write their reflections and feelings about the project (frustration, satisfaction) in their notebooks or portfolios.

Constructing With Recyclable Materials

Description. "Hands-on technology" is an exciting result of technological problem solving when students develop and construct their own "best" solution. This middle school activity moves beyond conducting experiments or finding solutions to word problems (all students doing the same task at the same time). In "hands-on technology," students are not shown a solution. Typically, this results in some very creative designs.

Using the tools and materials found in many schools, students design and construct solutions that allow them to apply the process skills. The products they create and engineer often use a wide range of materials, such as plastic, wood, and electrical supplies. During the course of solving a problem, students are forced to test hypotheses and frequently generate new questions. This involves much scientific investigation and mathematical problem solving, but it is quite different from routine classroom tasks. In this activity, a problem is introduced to the class. Working in small groups of four or five students, the challenge is to plan a way of coming up with a solution. Students are to document the steps they used along the way. Some suggestions: brainstorm, discuss with friends, draw pictures, show design ideas, use mathematics, present technical drawings, work together, or consult with experts.

Background Information. The best construction materials are strong yet lightweight. Wood is unexpectedly strong for its weight and therefore well suited for many structures. Larger buildings often use steel-reinforced concrete beams rather than wood in their construction. However, steel and concrete are both heavy, presenting problems in construction. A lighter material would be a great alternative and a best-seller in the construction industry. This could be done by reinforcing the beam with a material other than steel—ideally, a recyclable material.

The Problem. Design the lightest and strongest beam possible by reinforcing concrete with one or more recyclable materials: aluminum cans, plastic milk jugs, plastic soda bottles, and/or newspaper. Students must follow the construction constraints. The beam will be weighed, then it will be tested by supporting it at each end, and a load will be applied to the middle. The load will be increased until the beam breaks. The load divided by the beam's weight will give the load-to-weight ratio. The group designing the beam with the highest load-to-weight ratio will be awarded the contract.

Construction Limits. The solution must (a) be made into a reusable mold that the student designs, (b) result in a 40 cm (approximately 16 in.) beam that fits within a volume of 1,050 cubic centimeters (approximately 64 cubic inches), and (c) be made from concrete and recyclable materials.

Objectives. Groups of students will plan and design a beam, work on construction plans, and construct the beam. Students will gather information from a variety of resources and make sketches of all the possibilities they considered, then they will record the scientific principles they used.

Procedures. Divide students into small groups of three or four. Present the problem to the class. Students will discuss and draw out plans for how to construct a beam, design a concrete beam reinforced with recycled materials, and work together to construct, measure, and test the beam. Students will then present their invention to the class.

Evaluation. Students will document their work in a portfolio that includes sketches of all the possibilities their group considered, a graphic showing how their invention performed, descriptions of the process skills used in their solution, information and notes gathered from resources, and their thoughts and reflections about this project.

Stretching Thinking Skills
In Language Arts

Objective. This activity will develop students' critical and creative thinking skills.

Materials. Paper, pencil or pen, television screen, videodisc programs like MediaMax and Voyager Videostack. If these are not available, words can be written on the chalkboard.

Procedures. The television screen displays an image and a word. Students must write down one way in which the word and the picture are alike and one way that they are different. Students can share answers when the program is finished.

Evaluation and Follow-up. The class receives a list of the words that have been presented and is asked to write a story using at least half of them. If the school cannot provide CD-ROM technology, allow students to use resources like atlases, almanacs, and encyclopedias to search for ideas. When they have completed the activity, students should read their stories to the class.

Applying Computer
Problem Solving

Adding computer software to the problem-solving curriculum gives students a wider variety of practice situations. Use Muppet: Mix and Match (Sunburst) or a similar software package.

Instructional Activities. Introduce students to problem-solving strategies. Create two characters. Record the body, head, and feet chosen to make each one. Name each character and share results with other students. Create as many different creatures as possible in 10 minutes. Record the names. Make a list of all the characters the class found.

Evaluation. In a notebook, students should develop a plan to create all the possible characters and then share this with the class. Have students decide how the groups could cooperate to create all the characters. Encourage students to complete the project on the computer.

Using Math Skills in a
Stock Market Project

This activity utilizes the *process skills* of observing, inferring, classifying, measuring, comparing, sequencing, gathering and recording data, using language, sharing, predicting, and estimating.

Purpose and Objective. This activity serves a cross-curricular purpose by integrating mathematics, language arts, and social studies. Students will practice addition, subtraction, multiplication, and division by tracking the progress of the stock they "purchased." Students will explain rudimentary information about the formation of corporations, the economy, and the stock exchange.

Materials. A worksheet to record information, the business section of the daily newspaper (use the newspaper that reflects stock market changes in decimals), and calculators.

Procedures

1. Provide students with basic information on the formation of corporations (shares of stock sold to raise capital, election of corporate officers, investments made as a means to increase corporate capital).

2. Ask students to divide into groups (no fewer than two and no more than four in each group). They should select a name for the corporation they are forming and then elect or select corporate officers: president, vice-president, secretary, and treasurer. Each group should receive one work sheet and record its corporate name and officers.

3. Distribute copies of the business section of the daily newspaper. Help students to locate the New York Stock Exchange page. Ask each group to select one stock from the NYSE that they "purchase" with an imaginary $20,000.

4. Students should then extract information from the NYSE section of the paper, carefully using decoding skills, and accurately transpose that information to a work sheet. This task will enhance students' literary decoding skills.

5. Students should find the price per share of the stock they selected and divide that amount by 20,000. The quotient will determine how many shares they purchased. Provide students with very basic information about the stock (i.e., information regarding the effect of the NYSE on the economy).

6. Students should record all pertinent information on their work sheets. The work sheet is self-explanatory.

7. Each day students are to record their gains or losses on their work sheets. They may only sell their stock to purchase other stock after holding onto their stock for at least one month. This is to mimic the Securities and Exchange Act in miniature form (the SEA requires a six month hold for most investors) and it is also considered prudent investing to "ride out" the "bull" and "bear" markets.

Stock Market Work Sheet

Name of Corporation _____

President _____

Vice-President _____

Secretary _____

Treasurer _____

What stock did your corporation purchase?

At how much per share?

How many shares did you buy?

How much capital do you have left from your original $20,000?

Figure 4-3. Stock Market Work Sheet

Evaluation, Completion, and Follow-up. Students' consistent recording and daily tracking of changes in their stock will reflect their understanding. As time passes, students will become curious about the NASDAQ and may want to extend their investments. Teachers may want to present each group with an additional imaginary $20,000 to invest in other exchanges. Students will also ask questions about how someone can invest money in stock if he has much less than $20,000. This is an excellent time to introduce mutual funds. This may be a better second investment.

Going on a Shopping Spree With Calculators

This activity is for middle school mathematics and economics. It utilizes the process skills of observing, inferring, classifying, measuring, comparing, sequencing, gathering and recording data, using language, sharing, predicting, and estimating.

Materials. An envelope, thick squares of cloth, thin triangles of cloth, and a calculator.

Problem. Einstein's Clothing store is having a fantastic going-out-of-business sale. Anything that shoppers can fit into their envelope "shopping bag" is theirs for $75. Jackets are regularly priced at $200, pants and shirts normally sell for $25. The trick is to be able to glue the bag shut. Jackets are represented by the thick square pieces of cloth, pants and skirts are represented by the thin triangles.

Procedures. Provide students with the story of Einstein's going-out-of-business sale. Ask them to divide into groups (two to four per group). Each group is faced with three jobs: to get the most pieces of clothing in their bag, to have the lowest average price per item of clothing, and to save the most money off the regular price. They should then fill out Figure 4-4.

Shopping Spree Work Sheet

Number of items in your shopping bag _____.

Average price per item (divide 75 by the total number of items)

Total regular price (add the price of each item) _____.

Shopping spree savings (subtract 75 from the total regular price)_____.

Figure 4-4. Shopping Spree Worksheet

Evaluation and Follow up. Compare each group's answers with those of other members of the class.

Creating a Salt Volcano— Discovering Density

Objectives. Students will discover which is lighter: water or oil. This activity uses the process skills of observing, inferring, classifying, measuring, comparing, gathering and recording data, using language, sharing, predicting, estimating, and experimenting.

Background Information. Water is denser than oil, and salt is heavier than water. When these substances are mixed together, the oil sits on top of the water until the salt is added. Then the salt sinks to the bottom, carrying the oil with it.

Materials. Glass jar, water, salt, oil, food coloring.

Procedures. Pour about 3 inches of water into the jar, then pour about ¹/₃ cup of vegetable oil into the jar. Add one drop of food coloring if desired. Shake salt on top of the oil while counting slowly to 5. Record what happens.

Results. Students will explore the world of density by mixing the oil, water, and salt. Students will learn how and why liquids separate from each other.

Evaluation. In their journals, students should write about density and how the liquids separated from each other and why.

Understanding Surface Tension

Students will develop an understanding that technological solutions to problems, such as phosphate-containing detergents, have intended benefits and may have unintended consequences.

Objective. Students apply their knowledge of surface tension. This experiment shows how water acts as if it has a stretchy skin because water molecules are strongly attracted to each other. Students will also be able to watch how soap molecules squeeze between the water molecules, pushing them apart and reducing the water's surface tension.

This activity uses the process skills of observing, inferring, classifying, measuring, comparing, gathering and recording data, using language, sharing, predicting, estimating, and experimenting.

Background Information. Milk, which is mostly water, has surface tension. When the surface of milk is touched with a drop of soap, the surface tension of the milk is reduced at that spot. Since the surface tension of the milk at the soapy spot is much weaker than it is throughout the rest of the milk, the water molecules elsewhere in the bowl pull water molecules away from the soapy spot. The movement of the food coloring reveals these currents in the milk.

Materials. Milk (only whole or 2% will work), newspapers, a shallow container, food coloring, dishwashing soap, a saucer or a plastic lid, and toothpicks.

Procedures.
1. Take the milk out of the refrigerator ¹/₂ hour before the experiment starts.

2. Place the dish on the newspaper and pour about $1/2$ inch of milk into the dish.

3. Let the milk sit for 1–2 minutes.

4. Near the side of the dish, put one drop of food coloring in the milk. Place a few colored drops in a pattern around the dish. What happens?

5. Pour some dishwashing soap into the plastic lid. Dip the end of the toothpick into the soap, and touch it to the center of the milk. What happens?

6. Dip the toothpick into the soap again, and touch it to a blob of color. What happens?

7. Rub soap over the bottom half of a food coloring bottle. Stand the bottle in the middle of the dish. What happens?

8. The colors can move for about 20 minutes when students keep dipping the toothpick into the soap and touching the colored drops.

Follow-up Evaluation. Students will discuss their findings and share their outcomes with other groups.

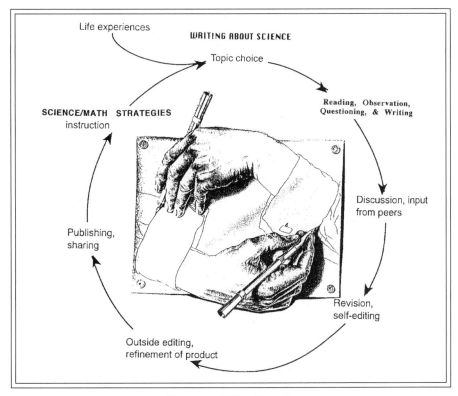

Figure 4-5. Writing About Science
(Digitalized image including elements from a painting by M. C. Escher.)

Examining Physics and Geometry With Geodesic Gumdrops

This activity is taken from the Exploratorium Website by Celeste Dizon.

Materials. A bag of gumdrops. (If gumdrops aren't available, try mini-marshmallows, clay, or larger jellied candy, cut up. Be creative.) A box of round toothpicks.

Basic Science Principles. Even though the gumdrop structures are standing absolutely still, their parts are constantly pulling and pushing on each other. Structures, even large ones, remain standing because some parts are being pulled or stretched while other parts are being pushed or squashed. The parts being pulled are in tension. The parts being squashed are in compression. Things that don't squash easily are strong in compression. Things that don't break when stretched are strong in tension. Some materials are strong in both tension and compression.

Another principle that helps to explain standing structures is the shape. Students may have noticed that squares collapse easily under compression, but triangles don't. Ask students if they know why this is so. It is because a square changes shape under compression into a diamond. The only way to change a triangle shape under compression is to break one of the sides.

Have students build the following structures:

Squares and Cubes

1. Start with four toothpicks and four gumdrops. Poke the toothpicks into the gumdrops to make a square with a gumdrop at each corner.

2. Put another toothpick into the top of each toothpick and gumdrop corner. Connect the gumdrops with toothpicks to make a cube.

3. Use more toothpicks and gumdrops to keep building squares onto the sides of the cube. When your structure is about 6 inches wide, try wiggling it from side to side. Does it feel solid, or is it kind of shaky?

Triangles and Pyramids

1. Start with three gumdrops and three toothpicks. Poke the toothpicks into the gumdrops to make a triangle with a gumdrop at each point.

2. Poke another toothpick into the top of each gumdrop. Bend

those three toothpicks toward the center. Poke all three toothpicks into one gumdrop to make a three-sided pyramid. (A three-sided pyramid has a triangle on each side. It takes four gumdrops and six toothpicks.)

3. Use more toothpicks and gumdrops to keep building triangles onto the sides of each pyramid. When the structure is about 6 inches wide, try wiggling it from side to side. Does it feel solid, or is it kind of shaky?

Four-Sided Pyramids

A big structure can be made out of squares and cubes, but it will be wiggly and probably fall down. If a structure is made only of triangles and pyramids, it won't be wiggly. A four-sided pyramid has a square bottom and triangles on all four sides. When a structure is built that uses both triangles and squares, the big structure will be more solid.

1. Build a square, then poke a toothpick into the top of each corner.

2. Bend all four toothpicks into the center and connect them with one gumdrop to make a four-sided pyramid.

3. What other ways can students use squares and triangles together?

4. The students can continue their exploration by building structures that combine triangles and squares and by looking at structures they encounter that use squares and triangles.

Measuring Body Ratios

Children need direct concrete experiences when interacting with mathematical ideas. The following activities are designed to clarify many commonly held incorrect ideas:

Finding the Ratio of One's Height to One's Head

How many times would a piece of string equal to a person's height wrap around that person's head? Many children have a mental picture of their bodies, and they make a guess relying on that perception. Have students make an estimate, then have them verify it for themselves. Few make an accurate guess based on their perceptions.

Comparing Height With Circumference

Have students imagine a soft drink can, then have them think about taking a string and wrapping it around the can to measure its circumference. Have students guess if the circumference is longer, shorter, or about the same height as the can. Encourage students to estimate how high the measure will reach. Then have the students try it.

As in the previous activity, many students guess incorrectly. The common misperception is that the string will be about the same length as the height of the can. There is a feeling of surprise or mental confusion when they discover that the circumference is about three times the height of the can. Repeat the experiment with other cylindrical containers. Have students record their predictions and come up with a conclusion.

Reviewing the Process Skills

The process skills are tools that enable students to gather and discover data for themselves. The major goals outlined in this chapter are discovering, communicating, and exploring. Some of the skills used to meet these goals include observing, inferring, classifying, measuring, comparing, sequencing, recording, predicting, estimating, and experimenting. To learn the processes, students investigate a variety of subject-matter contexts with concrete materials and are guided in their thinking with questions for each process.

In observing, students learn to use all of their senses, note similarities and differences in objects, and be aware of change. In classifying, students group things by properties or functions; they may also arrange them in some sense of order. Sequencing is part of this ordering system. Measuring teaches students to find or estimate quantity. Measurement is often applied in combination with skills in an integrated mathematics program. Communicating involves students in organizing information in some clear form that other people can understand. Recording, graphing, using maps, tables, and charts contribute to the communication process. The skill of inferring requires students to interpret or explain their observations. When students infer from data what they think will happen, often the term *predicting* is used.

The most challenging process, one that usually takes place with students in fourth grade and up, is experimentation. This process is divided into the following subskills: forming hypotheses, identifying variables, collecting data, analyzing data, and explaining outcomes.

The views about the inquiry processes and the examples presented in this chapter are built on several beliefs about content areas (Neuman, 1993):

1. Inquiry and process skills are used by adults to explore the mysteries of the universe.

2. Students who actively participate in understanding the interdisciplinary content must know how this knowledge is created.

3. Content becomes meaningful for elementary students when they understand the inquiry processes and are able to apply them.

4. The process skills play an important role in thinking across the curriculum.

Reaching Across Disciplines With Thematic Units

Themes are an effective way to connect the "big ideas" of various subjects to historical, social, and personal issues, as more than facts and isolated concepts, they link the structures of various disciplines. A *fact* is a statement based on evidence and observations, and a *concept* usually involves several facts. Themes integrate these concepts with facts, and makes any subject more relevant to real-life situations.

The spirit of inquiry can be strengthened in thematic lessons. It is important to broadly define the content that the students need to know in order to become informed, confident, and competent. Research supports the use of such integrated inquiry techniques to achieve higher levels of thinking and to make learning more meaningful. Such an approach is viewed as a way of teaching and of organizing instruction so that selected elements of subject matter are related to each other.

1. *Systems, Order, and Interactions.* A system (the number system, the education system) is an organized collection of objects of concepts that can have some influence on one another and appear to constitute a unified whole (Rutherford & Ahlgren, 1990). Students can form an understanding of order in systems. There is a sense of regularity by which events can be predicted and described. Learners then can develop understandings of basic principles, laws, theories, or models to explain the world.

2. *Evidence, Models, and Explanations.* A model is a simple representation that helps others to understand the concept better, such as a pump representing the heart.

3. *Constancy, Change, and Measurement Constancy.* This refers to ways in which systems do not change (a state of equilib-

rium). Change is important for understanding and predicting what will happen.

4. *Evolution and Equilibrium.* The idea of evolution is that the present arises from the forms of the past.

5. *Energy, Form, and Function.* Energy is a central concept of the physical sciences that pervades mathematical, biological, and geological sciences because it underlies any system of interactions. For example, in chemical terms, energy provides the basis for reactions between compounds.

6. *Language and Language Structure.* Language is the most powerful available tool we have for communicating our thoughts, defining our culture, and representing ourselves. The study of the systems and structures of language conventions allows students to apply their knowledge, gain experience, and adapt language to different tasks and audiences.

7. *Reading.* Reading a wide range of texts and literature is part of science and language learning, giving students new perspectives on their experiences and allowing them to discover how literature can make their lives richer and more meaningful.

8. *Researching.* As students ask questions, pose problems, and generate ideas concerning language and science, they accumulate, analyze, and evaluate data from many sources to communicate information and their discoveries for a specific purpose.

Thematic inquiry can be used to integrate concepts and facts throughout all areas of the curriculum, but some science educators are concerned that the usual curricular divisions of Earth, life, and physical science may be diminished. The same concerns are voiced by language arts classroom teachers. However, just the opposite is true.

As disciplines rapidly expand, a thematic approach serves as a powerful way of uniting or transferring knowledge from one field to the next. If these connections are successful, then these intellectual habits should carry over and enrich other fields and disciplines. As a result, students may more clearly see the overall purpose and logic of the educational system. Thus, an integrative approach to inquiry will not only help them to develop a meaningful structure for understanding science and language arts but also to see the relationship to other subjects and their daily lives.

Developing an Interdisciplinary Thematic Unit

The interdisciplinary thematic aspect of today's literacy builds on the way that citizens actually use language and the scientific method to study the natural world much as scientists do. In this way, teachers can examine themes by applying methods and language from different disciplines to examine an issue, problem, experience, or central theme. Attacking a broad topic with the intellectual tools of several fields stimulates critical thinking skills and can easily allow for learning through social interaction. Motivation can be intensified when student interest is central to the choice of theme or problem to explore.

A thematic unit is more than a collection of lesson plans. It should be viewed as a dynamic inquiry project. The basic goals are set ahead of time through a joint teacher-student effort. The steps to a thematic unit include the following.

1. *Selecting a Theme.* This should be challenging and related to real-world concerns. By building on the students' existing knowledge, an interdisciplinary thematic unit must be rich enough to hold interest for at least a week. This means connecting student interests to the curriculum in a manner that allows for the development of those interests and of academic skills.

2. *Deciding on a Desired Outcome.* Unit outcomes should be decided in advance. These may relate to cognitive skills (comprehending concepts), or social development (working in groups).

3. *Mapping and Brainstorming.* This stage of idea collection and organization can include using graphic organizers to outline the major activities for each subject area or brainstorming. In mapping, you simply put the main idea in the middle and have spokes coming out on four or five main points. Like smaller branches off tree limbs, less central ideas sprout out on the paper.

4. *Making a Time line.* As the key decision maker, the teacher determines the length of time for each activity and learning experience.

5. *Reviewing Concepts and Skills.* List the concepts and skills that will be part of the process.

6. *Providing Resources.* Outline what material everybody needs.

7. *Connecting Learning Centers and Bulletin Boards.* These can serve as vehicles for reaching unit outcomes. An interactive bulletin board can connect to e-mail or even the Internet.

8. *Summarizing with a Cumulative Activity.* At this point students should be able to synthesize what they have gained from the various disciplinary tools applied to the problem.

9. *Having an Assessment Plan.* Use performance assessment, portfolios, conferences, anecdotes, and exams. At the very least, an informal evaluation should be used to foster improve the next time around.

10. *Including Daily Lesson Plans.* Lesson plans must have specific descriptions, including objectives, rationale, concepts,

materials, and procedures; change as needed.

When thematic units are participatory, rich in content, and related to student interest, they can inspire enthusiasm in both the teacher and the class.

The activities presented here are designed to give students a chance to thoroughly explore concepts that cross disciplines. Each activity focuses students' attention on an interesting event or method. Materials and step-by-step directions for the activity are provided. Occasionally, some information or instructional method is added within the procedures to help clarify the students' experience. An assessment section is included in most activities; performance assessment offers opportunities to inquire and learn more about a topic.

A background information section in some of the activities provides necessary information or notes to help the teacher. The goal is to provide teachers with background experiences that will aid in building a repertoire of strategies, activities, and skills for teaching science and language arts content to children.

Sample Thematic Activity: Rocks

There are many questions about how life first evolved. One way we can trace the history of the Earth is to teach about the processes that explain the origin of rocks and their changes.

Finding Out About Rocks

Language arts and writing skills are emphasized in this introduction to a unit on rocks. For this activity, students bring a rock to class. They get to know their rock by describing it to someone else. They touch their rock, then pass it to the teacher. The teacher collects the rocks in a box, then the teacher passes the rocks back. The students must get in a circle, put their hands behind their backs and pass the rocks to the person next to them. They should not look at the rock in their hand.

If they think the rock they hold is theirs, they can take a peek. If this is correct, they take their rock and sit down. This continues until all students have found their own rock. Students then do guided imagery or a visualization activity (see below). After the visualization students share what happened in their visualization. Students also write a poem about their rock. This activity uses the process skills of observing, inferring, classifying, measuring, comparing, gathering and recording data, using language, sharing, predicting, estimating, and experimenting. The themes involved are evidence, models, explanations, and systems.

Engaging Students in Guided Imagery Experiences

For this activity, the teacher guides students through an imaginary journey, encouraging them to create images or mental pictures and ideas. Students close their eyes and imagine that they are walking in a lush green forest along a trail. While walking, they notice a rock along the trail and pick it up. The students imagine that they are very tiny, so tiny that they become smaller than the rock. They imagine crawling around on the rock, using their hands and feet to hold onto the rock as they scale its surface. They feel the rock. (Is it rough or smooth? Can they climb it easily?) They smell the rock. (What does it smell like?) They look around. (What does the rock look like? Is there anything unusual about the rock?) When the students are ready, they make themselves large and come back to the classroom, open their eyes, and share their experience.

Afterwards students discuss their experiences in groups, writing on a computer, or creating a multimedia artistic expression. For example, on the computer, instruct students to make a list of as many observations as they can. Then direct them to write a Japanese poem following these directions:

Line 1: Identify the object.

Line 2: Write an observation of the object.

Line 3: Tell your feeling about the object.

Line 4: Write another observation about the object.

Line 5: End with a synonym for the name of the object.

This utilizes the process skills of observing, inferring, classifying, measuring, comparing, recording, gathering data, using language, sharing, predicting, estimating, and experimenting. The themes involved are language, language structure, reading, systems, and patterns of change.

Graphic Organizers Help to Connect Process Skills and Themes

Many students learn more when they can graphically represent relationships with webs, maps, time lines, and data charts. Graphic organizers (Figure 4-6), followed by a little time for reflection, can help students to remember and retain what they learn. Concepts can be associated and learning consolidated during small group work that is followed by periods of purposeful processing time.

A practical example: Organize groups of two or three to use felt-tip pens to construct relationships on a large piece of paper and present the results to the whole class. The main idea is put in a circle in the middle, with secondary ideas stemming out to the side (Figure 4-7). This step allows a minute or two for reflection and cognitive processing after each concept has been covered. It is also a good idea to have students put a brief reflective comment in a personal journal.

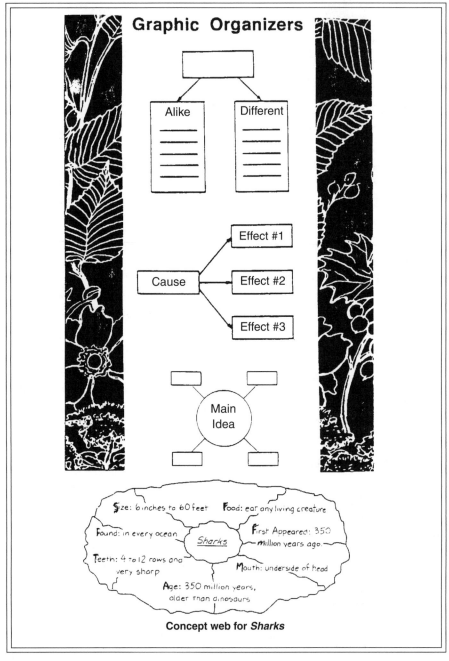

Figure 4-6. Graphic Organizers

Process Skills Connect Content Across the Curriculum

Students clearly benefit when process-oriented approaches to instruction are used across the curriculum. Teachers who carefully attend to process skills usually work within a constructivist environment where learning is viewed as an active endeavor strongly influenced by social dynamics. The emphasis is on inquiries into topics of study in which students take ownership of learning tasks and collaborate in a risk-free setting. Within this context, students benefit by learning to recognize how writers relate ideas through cause-effect, comparison-contrast, and problem-solution.

It certainly helps to have the ability to decode, interpret, and analyze visual symbols across a variety of disciplines. As teachers find natural connections between subjects, they can take steps to harness the appropriate technology so that students can amplify and communicate the results in a way that allows them to apply what they have learned in their day-to-day lives.

It is important to remind ourselves that our visions do matter. The visions we develop and offer our children really do help to shape the future.

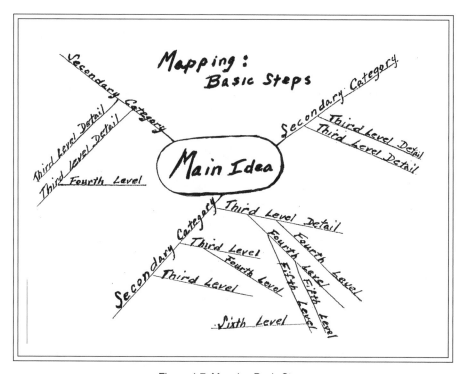

Figure 4-7. Mapping Basic Steps

References

Abruscato, J. (2001). *Teaching children science: Discovery methods for the elementary and middle grades.* Needham Heights, MA: Allyn & Bacon.

Applebee, A. N. (1991). Environments for language teaching and learning: Contemporary issues and future directions. In J. Flood, J. M. Jenson, D. Lapp, & J. R. Squire (Eds.), *Handbook of research for teaching the English language arts* (pp. 549–556). New York: Macmillan.

Bruner, J. (1961, Winter). The act of discovery. *Harvard Educational Review 31*, 21–32.

Hamm, M. (1992). Achieving scientific literacy through a curriculum connected with mathematics and technology. *School Science and Mathematics 92* (1), 6–9.

Hurd, P. D. (2000). *Transforming middle school science education.* New York: Teachers College Press.

Lundau, B. (Ed.). 2000. *Perception, cognition, and language.* Cambridge, MA: MIT Press.

Martin, D. J. (2000). *Elementary science methods: A constructivist approach.* (2nd ed.). Belmont, CA: Wadsworth/Thomas Learning.

Meier, D. (2000). *Scribble scrabble—teaching children to become successful readers and writers.* New York: Falmer Press.

National Academy Press. (1996). *National science education standards.* Washington, DC: Author.

National Council for Accreditation of Teacher Education. (2000). *Technology and the new professional teachers: Preparing the 21st century classroom.* Washington, DC: Author.

National Council of Teachers of Mathematics. (2000). *Curriculum and evaluation standards for school mathematics.* Weston, VA: Author.

Neuman, D. (1993). *Experiencing Elementary Science.* Belmont, CA: Wadsworth.

Park, R. L. (1999, December 7). *Mars, still ours to conquer.* The New York Times, p. A31.

Reigeluth, C. (Ed.). (1999). *Instructional design theories and models: A new paradigm of intructional theory.* Mahwah, NJ: Erlbaum.

Roblyer, M. D., Edwards, J., & Havriluk, M. A. (1997). *Integrating educational technology into teaching.* Columbus, OH: Merrill.

Rutherford, F. J., & Ahlgren, A. (1990). *Science for all Americans.* New York: Oxford University Press.

Sagan, C. (1994). *Pale blue dot.* New York: Random House.

Van de Walle, J. (1997). *Elementary and middle school mathematics.* White Plains, NY: Macmillan.

 # Technological Literacy: Teaching, Learning, Culture, and Technology

Any means of communication interferes directly with common outward reality, the everyday reality and, therefore, with the common prose of life.

—*Hegel*

Technology-mediated American mass culture is sweeping the globe and changing ways of life, for better or worse. The inescapable march began with the movies and continued with television. Now newer information and communication technologies have done an even more thorough job of capturing diverse cultural expressions within their domains. The United States successfully markets programming for television, computers, video games, and the Internet. In the new tightly wired world of the 21st century, the soft power of our technology, culture, and commerce is bound to have hard effects.

Strangely, the technology has managed to go a long way toward homogenizing popular culture around the world while contributing to the cultural fragmentation of America. By the 1990s, American television had splintered domestic audiences with channels aimed at every possible demographic, cultural, language, and interest group. Except for special circumstances, the idea of a mass audience is a thing of the past. The Internet has vastly accelerated the fragmentation process. Now even the most narrowly demented have virtual groups that they can join.

In spite of the potential interactivity and diversity of contents, electronic media messages tend to follow a common cognitive pattern. In this country we have found that when extended family ties, old neighborhoods, and communities are weakened by isolated suburbs, people are more likely to turn to the media for ideas, standards, advice, and entertainment. In all its forms, communication technology has been found to have a powerful ability to process thought and change how we perceive reality.

The technology of the early 21st century is astonishing, strange, and reshaping every aspect of our lives. A prime ingredient in today's media revolution is information technology. A little like yesterday's television programming, it is reshaping the social landscape around the world. It is little wonder that today's media realities have created a need for new, technology-based literacies. To emphasize the positive possibilities, American democracy depends on having citizens who can engage in the technological debate. We must all participate in planning this compelling adventure, or today's technology could turn into a high-tech version of what was said about Lord Byron: mad, bad, and dangerous to know.

Taking advantage of enabling communication possibilities requires us to consider how new technological literacies redefine our interaction with each other and our relationship to the world. It is counterproductive to get drawn too far into the confusing debate over how to define terms like *media literacy, technology literacy*, or *networking literacy*. Some writers refer to computer, network, and technology literacies as *tool literacies*. Others group information, visual, and media literacy as *literacies of representation*. Many industrialized countries have included all of the nonprint communication-related literacies under the *media literacy* umbrella and embedded the subject in the basic curriculum. Canada, England, Australia, and Germany are just four examples of countries that have mandated media education and view it as a powerful associate of print literacy.

Technology-Mediated Literacies and the Curriculum

> Technology literacy is a complex, integrated process involving people, procedures, ideas, devices, and organization for analyzing problems and devising, implementing, evaluating, and managing solutions to those problems, involving all aspects of learning.
>
> —Association for Educational Communications and Technology

The successful educational use of any medium is highly dependent on the context in which it is used. Linking technology with standards-based reform involves clarifying educational goals and reconceptualizing how literacy and learning activities are orchestrated. The best approach is to establish clear educational goals, then use the best mix of technology to achieve those goals. Television, computers, the Internet, and integrated information systems are all things that students need to understand and master. Comprehension, analysis, and production skills are important to today's literacy, but the content of the curriculum is always more important than mastering specific software or hardware.

Figure 5-1. The Continuous Flow of Computer Code

When children grow up with computers at home, they are less inclined to accept instruction that is less interesting than what they can experience outside school. The role of the teacher is bound to change along with media changes in the home and school environment. However, learning will still depend on what humans do best: role modeling, nurturing, and lighting intellectual fires. Technology can assist us with project-based learning and give us exciting access to information, but it takes good teachers to be sure that it actually amplifies learning.

Schools, students, and technology have changed significantly over the last decade, but teachers are still at the heart of instruction. To prepare students in a new century, teachers need ongoing opportunities to be as informed and inspiring as possible. Only when teachers are able to keep up-to-date and are capable of applying a thorough knowledge of effective instruction can we be sure that high-tech tools will actually help children to reach new plateaus of thinking and learning.

All of the standards projects mention technology as a partner in learning subject matter. The science standards go into the most detail. Science looks to both high and low technology to help students understand the laws of the physical and biological universe. Forming connections between the natural and technological worlds is viewed as important to understanding how technological objects and natural systems interact. In every subject, students can use electronic databases to retrieve information and examine the relationship between variables.

From interactive literature in the language arts to digital laboratories in mathematics, each subject in the core curriculum is building on promising high-tech possibilities.

Technology Samples From the Science Standards

Students Should Have an Understanding of Science and Technology

The science and technology standards connect students to the designed world and introduce them to the laws of nature through their understandings of how technological objects and systems work. People have always invented tools to help them solve problems and answer many questions that they have about their world. Science is one way of explaining the natural world; technology helps to explain the human-made (or designed) world. In the early grades, students can begin to differentiate between science and technology by understanding the similarities, differences, and relationships between the two. Observing, comparing, sorting, and classifying objects, both natural and manufactured, are skills that can be employed at this level. Just as scientists and engineers work in teams to get results, so too should students work in teams that combine scientific and engineering talents.

All Students Should Develop Abilities of Technological Design

This standard begins the understanding of the design process, as well as the ability to solve simple design problems. Children's abilities in technological problem solving can be developed by firsthand experience and by studying technological products and systems in their world. Young students should have experiences with objects they are familiar with and find out how these objects work. Experiments might include exploring simple household tools or kitchen items. Older students can enrich their understanding by designing something and studying technological products and systems. Suitable design tasks for students should be well-defined, based on contexts that are familiar in the home, school, and immediate community. By the time students reach middle school, investigations using technology can be complemented by activities in which the purpose is to solve a problem, meet a human need, or develop a product.

The science standards list a sequence of five stages that are usually involved in a technology-based problem solving process:

1. Identify and state the problem. Children should explain the problem in their own words and identify a specific task and solution.
2. Design an approach to solving the problem. This may involve building something or making something work better. Students should be able to describe and communicate their ideas.
3. Implement a proposed solution. Students should work individually and as a group using tools, techniques, and measurement devices where appropriate.
4. Evaluate results. Students evaluate their solutions as well as those of others by considering how well a product or design solved the problem.
5. Communicate the problem, design, and solutions. Students should include oral, written, and pictorial communication of the design process and product. Group discussions, written reports, pictures, or group presentations show their abilities.

Technology Samples From the Mathematics Standards

The National Council of Teachers of Mathematics (NCTM) standards include the use of technology in their set of core beliefs about students, teaching, learning, and mathematics.

The widespread impact of technology on nearly every aspect of our lives requires changes in the content and nature of school mathematics programs. The math standards suggest, in keeping with these changes, that students should be able to use calculators and computers to investigate mathematical concepts and increase their mathematical understanding.

Selected Technology Elements in the Language Arts Standards

Students use a variety of technological and informational resources to gather information and communicate knowledge. Students need to learn how to use many technologies, from computer networks to electronic mail and interactive video. Using computers and video technology empowers students to represent themselves to others. This experience gives them the power of visual representation and enables them to see its importance in enriching a sense of cultural identity.

Students participate in a reflective and critical literacy community. This includes "visual language." Whether students' participation in a community is between classmates or technologically mediated by computer networking and video, it is an essential part of their learning to view themselves as effective users of language and technology. Virtual book clubs represent one of the possibilities. Interactive cinematic narrative is another.

Students Should Understand the Role of Theatre, Film, Television, and Electronic Media in Their Community and Other Cultures

Students need many opportunities to analyze the role of theatre, film, television, and electronic media in their daily lives. This can be done through discussions, illustrations, drama, or writing.

Students should be able to apply media techniques and processes with skill, confidence, and sensitivity in their artworks. Working in the visual arts with a wide range of subject matter, symbols, meaningful images, and visual expressions, students extend their understanding and express their feelings and emotions. To achieve its positive potential, multimedia requires a solid background in the arts. Otherwise television, film, video games, and their media associates are more likely to indoctrinate our youth with a lot of tawdry visual trash. The technology makes bad art easier to mass produce.

Constructing Meaning Across the Curriculum

Whatever the task, literacy tools can magnify the ability to think and articulate our thoughts. They can also help us to act together on the result. Exploring the world and designing solutions to problems is most successful when students can use technological tools much the way adults use them. By using a variety of technologies for real-world inquiry, problem solving, and communicating, students can come to realize that learning is more than preparing for life, it is an ongoing part of life itself.

Student-generated questions provide excellent opportunities to apply a whole range of technological tools to interesting real-world problems. In the early elementary grades, many tasks can be designed around the familiar contexts of the home, school, and community. Figuring out the best ways to solve problems is most important. So low-tech or the nonelectronic possibilities should not be omitted. Although realistic problems usually have multiple solutions, it is often best for lower grade students when there are only one or two possible solutions. This cuts preparation time and complicated assembly. *Simplicity* and *elegance* are not contradictory terms.

Whatever the grade level, multidisciplinary analysis of problems is natural when it connects to the students' day-to-day world. Mixing virtual with face-to-face collaboration makes it more interesting. To some degree, communicational and informational technologies have always reflected the strengths and weaknesses of the human condition. They create and solve problems. In terms of problem solving, today's expanding mix of electronic media can serve as passports to an expanding reservoir of dynamic knowledge and communication. For this and other reasons, technology is in the process of redefining how we learn, play, and understand our lives. It is also redefining literacy and reshaping the nature of knowledge acquisition.

Designing a Communications Technology Time Line

Time is often a difficult concept for children to grasp. Throughout modern history people have recorded the passage of time.

This activity gets students involved in time measurement by using a number of old and new technological tools. The ways in which people communicate with each other have changed throughout history.

Students may use reference books, journals, communication devices from home, and information from their grandparents or community members. Have students research the history of communications technology and create a time line in their journal. Using as many actual objects or their representations, encourage students to assemble a communications time line project for display. Remind the students that each time period needs to have some examples of the actual objects used and a written explanation of these communications devices.

Reading Culture Through Advertising

Plan a lesson with a librarian. Use old magazines if they are available. Make copies of ads from each decade of this century. Much of this may be on microfilm. Some can be found on the Internet. Compare and contrast the images in the ads, then relate them to social events in each decade. Ask students to produce their own ads using a style they find from an earlier time—the 1920s, '30s, '40s, and so on. This can be done electronically or by simply sketching a one- or two-page storyboard.

Research can also be done on the history of cigarette advertising, misleading claims, and ad campaigns directed toward a specific audience. Focus on who was or is responsible for an ad. *The Standard Directory of Advertisers* will tell you the name and address of the advertising agency that created the ad.

Ask students to choose a recent advertisement that they think is offensive or one that they think represents things fairly. "Lemon" awards are given each year for the most irresponsible television ads in America. There are also international awards for the best ads. Students can write a letter of complaint or congratulations on a job well done.

Technology is changing everything, even itself. The Internet, for example, is changing how we view and use television. After a half-century of lumbering change, television technology has begun to change almost as fast as computer software. Narrowcasting to a small audience has overtaken broadcasting. TV is going digital and figuring out ways to work hand in hand with the Web, satellites, computers, and the telephone. Electronic media will continue to change itself, and it will change how we go about teaching and learning. From cable modems to WebTV, our choices and the technology itself will settle the communication conflicts. Converging technologies not only influence popular culture, but sooner or later (probably later) a mixture of powerful technology is going to influence the curriculum.

We must all take technology seriously. Teachers can use digital technology and its information and communication associates as a point of departure for collaborative inquiry. Digital tools are powerful vehicles for inquiry-based classrooms. The Internet is but one example; it can be used in real time or programs can be downloaded for later use. Students can gain access to data, new virtual experiences, lifelike simulations, and dynamic model building.

By altering the communication and information environments, our new technological tools give us the possibility for creating new knowledge. Integrated technology gives us instant access to scattered information that we can use to analyze trends, search out opportunities, and create knowledge. The result is transforming the social and educational environments before we have a chance to think carefully about why we want to use them and what we hope to accomplish. By the time we have one item figured out, the next version has already been released.

Learning Media Lessons From Television

Different communication modes often borrow codes from each other. We are all consumers of a wide range of media, and we must all learn to make critical judgments about the quality and usefulness of the electronic possibilities springing up around us. One way for students to become more media literate is to learn to "read" and "write" with media. Children can become adept at extracting meaning from the conventions of producing in any medium.

Like print, visual imagery from a computer or TV screen can be mentally processed at different levels of complexity. Certain notions of time, space, or morality are beyond children's grasp before certain developmental levels are reached (Figure 5-2). Vocabulary isn't the only thing that impedes children from grasping some adult content. Children may lack the fundamental integrative capacities to group certain kinds of information together meaningfully in ways that are obvious to adults. Thus, children who need help in developing strategies for tuning out televised irrelevancies may be especially vulnerable to unwanted adult content.

The greater the experiential background, the greater the base for the development of technological literacy. The ability to make subtle judgments about what is seen and heard is a developmental outcome that proceeds from stage to stage with an accumulation of critically informed viewing experiences. Thus, different age groups reveal various levels of comprehension when they interact with stories in any medium. An 8-year-old, for example, retains a relatively small proportion of the central actions, events, or settings found in a computer or video program. Even when they retain explicit content, younger children often fail to infer the connections between scenes.

Figure 5-2. "Mass Media and the Modern Classroom"

Meaning is constructed by each participant at many levels. Most of the time children construct meaning from television content without even thinking about it. They attend to stimuli and extract meaning from subtle messages. How well television content is understood varies according to the similarities between the viewers and the content, to the viewers' needs and interests, and to the age of the individual using a particular medium. The underlying message of most TV programs and many Internet functions is that viewers should consume as much as possible while changing as little as possible.

Broadcast television and the World Wide Web are prime examples of technological tools that provide us with a common culture. Unfortunately, that common culture often tends toward cynicism and selfishness. American mass media has a habit of responding to the public hunger for community with programming that applies market values and standards to human relationships. While one is immersed in mass media, this may be hard to discern, but living in community with others requires far more than attention to profits.

Sorting through the mass media themes of mental conservatism and material addition requires carefully developed thinking skills and social conscience. Building a culture of meaning is an increasingly difficult and varied undertaking. Understanding what is going on and learning how to create with a medium helps. On a more general level, poetry, literature, and public service are just three ways to temper the desire for personal gain with a little compassion, spirituality, and a few transcendent values. When we can all apply an informed set of analytical tools to the mass media signals washing over us, the prospects for our public life will improve dramatically.

Reflective thought, imaginative play, and peer interaction are important to child development. Technology matters, but it doesn't automatically add much to the instructional equation. Still, in a media-saturated world, children should be able to do enough active work with information and communication technology to make sense of the contents and utilize the possibilities. Evaluative activities include judging, assigning worth, assessing what is admired, and deciding what positive and negative impressions should be assigned to the content. Literacy in any medium is an enabling factor that permits critical accumulation, organization, retrieval, and systematic use.

Students learn best if they take an active role in their own learning. Relying upon a host of cognitive inputs, individuals select and interpret the raw data of experience to produce a personal understanding of reality. Ultimately it is up to each person to determine what to pay attention to and what to ignore. How elements are organized and how meaning is attached to any concept is an individual act that can be influenced by a number of external agents. The thinking that must be done to make sense of perceptions ultimately transforms the "real world" into different things for different people.

Literacy, Role Models, and Change

Literacy in all of its forms is a technology or a set of techniques for decoding, reproducing, and creating communications. The integration of electronic communication and the rise of interactive networks changes what it means to be literate in the 21st century. Once a literacy shift begins, it gathers its own momentum. Books are elegant user-friendly tools that won't go away, but technology-intensive mass media are now central shaping forces in our lives. Ours is the first society in history where many lives have, at least metaphorically, moved inside the media. We all have to make sense of the oral, print, and digital literacies in the context of our time.

Many of the skills applied to print media also apply to newer literacy tools. Some are particular to each medium. Digital communication forms are somewhat unique because they can combine spoken, written, and electronic codes and conventions into data that can converge gracefully into an interactive audiovisual experience. For schools, the challenge is to take the best practices for teaching developing multiple literacies and give teachers everywhere the resources they need to do the job.

The following activities can be used to understand the media in America:

1. Interview someone who has recently arrived in this country. Have Students ask them to describe what is different about American media and culture. This can be done as homework, or five recent immigrants can be invited to class one put with each small group of children.

2. Have students list the media they frequently deal with and note how much time they spend with each one. How would life be different if they were cut of from one (or all) of them?

3. Keep a log of advertisers or sponsors whose names appear on television. What connections can students make between sponsors, products, and the nature of the show itself?

4. Have students write a brief autobiography about how they learned to read, watch television, or use the Internet. Movies, compact discs, newspapers, and magazines are included. Discuss one medium or combine several.

Literacy can be used as an instrument of conformity or creativity. A rich literacy-intensive home and school environment helps to determine whether literacy is liberating or constraining. Communication technologies, literacy practices, and the need for educational renewal all contribute to change. Whatever the context, in an increasingly mediated world, modeling is very important.

Students watch teachers all the time. In many ways they learn as much from their school's routines and rituals as they do from their classes. Teachers cannot expect to be perfect but should at least be aware of what they are doing. Students learn from watching and listening. If teachers want students to become thoughtful, informed, and literate citizens, then teachers must model such traits. The same thing is true for literacy. If the adults in a child's life read and take a disciplined approach to their use of television and the Internet, then children are likely to do the same.

Parents, teachers, and other adults can significantly affect what information children gather from any medium. Students' social, educational, and family lives influence what messages they take from the various media. Communication and information technology give us complex, silent messages about the attitudes and values of culture. Messages from images and sound are at least as important as the words we read or hear. Becoming adept at comprehending media messages means being able to do the following:

- Understand the grammar and syntax as it is expressed in different forms
- Analyze the pervasive appeals of advertising
- Compare similar presentations or similar purposes in different media
- Identify values in language, characterization, conflict resolution, and sound or visual images
- Identify elements in dramatic presentations associated with the concepts of plot, theme, characterization, motivation, program format, and production
- Utilize strategies for the management of duration of viewing and program choices.

Parents and teachers can help by explaining content and showing how a media experience relates to a student's interests. Adults can also exhibit an informed response, point out misleading messages, and take care not to build curiosity for undesirable programming.

Informed parents can really make a difference. The habits of families play a large role in determining how children approach any medium. For example, the reactions of parents and siblings toward programming messages all have a large influence on the children. If there are books, magazines, and newspapers around the house, children will pay more attention to print. Influencing how children conduct themselves with any medium requires certain rules about what may or may not be watched or what Web sites are acceptable. A simple suggestion: Put the computer with the Internet connection or the WebTV unit in the family room.

Television serves as an example for all media. Adults can influence the settings in which children watch TV. For example, turning the TV off during meals sets a family priority. Families can also seek a more open and equal approach to choosing television shows—interacting before, during, and after the program. Parents can also organize formal or informal activities outside the house that provide alternatives to TV viewing, video games, or Internet surfing. Set time limits for using any technology.

To foster understanding of media messages, teachers can capitalize on the information and knowledge that students bring to class. It is important to look more closely at the business side of the media. From all the selling and salaries involved, clearly the mass media is an economically valued storyteller in our society. Teachers can ask the following questions:

- What is your favorite Web site, TV show, and movie?
- What kind of information, show, or movie is it?
- What are the formal features of your choices?
- What are the most appealing elements of each?
- What do you know about how each medium constructs its "stories"?
- What are some of the formal and informal structures of the Internet, the movie industry, and TV broadcasting?
- What are the values in these mass-produced programs, and how do they change our shared experiences as a people?

How can we go about creating an instructional atmosphere that is enabled by the technology? Computers have been part of the lives of many people for a decade or two, but it is only recently that a large number of Americans have learned how to really use them. Computers and their technological associates are rarely used to compute anymore; they are used to communicate, gather information, simulate, and explore. Every day many students are receiving and sending large volumes of text, images, and sound. The next step is to sort through the glut and construct some knowledge.

One of the major goals of any educational innovation is to make subjects comprehensible, more interesting, and more connected to everyday life. When it comes to schooling, this means connecting to what the curriculum is trying to accomplish and making sure that students don't mind facing lifelong learning needs. Technology can support real-world concepts with visual imagery and help students to actually see and share problems. Something very special happens when students know that their research (images and print) is available to other students around the world. The same can be said of the special appeal of bringing images, text, and sound from the outside world into isolated classrooms. It is important to remember that learning is more about mental models than it is about imagery.

A Media Scavenger Hunt—
Exploring the Technology

Give students a one-page scavenger-hunt activity in which they have to find everything from the atomic number of uranium to DNA research to how to say "hello" to people in Finland.

Find some current information that you believe and explain it. Then find something about current events that you don't believe and explain why. Examine the validity of something hard to believe—in the newspaper, on TV, or on the Web.

Critique a movie, computer program or Web site. Ask some questions about the content. (Come up with some answers and learn to ask better questions.) How would the accuracy of information from an advertisement be compared to information found on a Web site such as that of *National Geographic?*

Each Medium Uses Its
Own Distinctive Technology

Each communication medium makes use of its own distinctive technology for gathering, encoding, sorting, and conveying its contents associated with different situations. The technological mode of a medium affects the interaction with its users, just as the method for transmitting content affects the knowledge acquired. Learning is affected by the delivery system and by what is delivered. The quality of the programming and the level of interactivity are the keys to success.

Processing must always take place, and it always requires skill. The closer the match between the way information is presented and the way it can be mentally represented, the easier it is to learn. Better communication means easier processing and more transfer. More than a decade ago research suggested that voluntary attention and the formation of ideas can be facilitated by electronic media, with concepts becoming part of a child's repertoire. New educational choices are being opened by new electronic technologies. The impulse to use technology to somehow increase productivity and reduce the cost of education rarely works, because no technology replaces good teachers. The question is how to use the technology to support these teachers and do something really worthwhile for education, culture, and society.

We are now at a stage where even novices can find their way around global networks—downloading images, messages, audio, and video with the click of a mouse. The Internet has become an example of how a virtual community can connect telecommunicators around the world. It is also an example of frenzied commercialization. Across media platforms, the next few years will be a critical time for building things into communications media that benefit the public. If we leave everything to market forces, the results will be much worse than on commercial television. It is time to consciously attend to the role of mass communications in a democratic society.

Educators are increasingly looking to technology as they strive to make their classrooms more dynamically interactive, collaborative, and student centered. As we put together the technological components that provide access to a set of active learning experiences, it is important to develop a modern philosophy of teaching, learning, and social equity. For example, although new communication technology has the potential to make society more equal, it has the opposite effect when access is limited to those with the money for the equipment. Schools, libraries, and public-private partnerships can help turn this around. As we enter a world of computers, camcorders, interactive TV, the Web, databases, and satellite technology, the schools are behind, and now is the time for them to start catching up with the more technologically sophisticated institutions.

Electronically connecting the human mind to global information resources will result in a shift in human consciousness similar to the change that occurred when a society moved from an oral to a written culture. The challenge is to make sure that this information is available for everyone in a 21st-century version of the public library. The technology could give us the ability to impact the tone and priorities of gathering information and learning in a democratic society. Of course, every technology has the potential for both freedom and domination. As with other technological advances, this one can mirror back to us all sides of the human condition. If we are headed in the wrong direction, technology won't help us to get to the right place.

There is no doubt about the fact that the world is reengineering itself with many technological processes. The convergence of information and communication technologies may be the one of the codes to transform the learning process and make people more creative, resourceful, and innovative in the things they do, but we mustn't expect technology alone to turn things around. While we learn to use what's available today, we also need to start building a social and educational infrastructure that can travel the knowledge highways of the future. Experts may disagree about the ultimate consequences of innovation in electronic learning, but the development of basic skills, mental habits, wisdom, and character traits will be increasingly affected by the technology.

Navigating the Crosscurrents of Technological Change

Information and communication technology should be integrated into our lives in ways that support and generate deep urges to learn and to teach. The best results occur when informed educators, rather than the technology itself, drive the change. Sailing through the crosscurrents of a technological age means harmonizing the present and the future. (Figure 5-3). It means attending to support mechanisms, and it requires the development of habits of the heart and of the intellect. Thinking about the educational process has to precede thinking about the technology.

Rapid changes in information technology are resulting in fewer differences among the television screen, the computer screen, and telephone-linked networks. In fact, connecting a cable modem to the TV line results in much faster communication and quick acting full-motion video. When "online" means "on-cable," it becomes even easier to send and receive e-mails, participate in electronic chat groups, and quickly roam around the Web. Within a few years, very broad bandwidths will result in much faster connections and high-quality video.

Possibilities for intelligent use of the computer-based technologies may be found in earlier media. For example, when television first gained a central place in the American consciousness, it was viewed as a neutral instrument in human hands. It is and does what people want. The same thing might be said about today's multimedia and telecommunications technologies. The Internet and other computer-controlled educational tools may have great promise, but anyone who thinks that technological approaches will solve the problems of our schools is mistaken.

The Internet is a high-tech example of how linked multimedia computers can help us to weave a new community—or waste a great deal of time. To have positive results, we need a clear set of educational priorities before we select the technologies to advance those priorities. The notion that positive things happen simply by putting the technology in the classrooms is wrong. The technology helps children to learn better only if it is part of an overall learning strategy.

It is important to remember that learning works best within the context of human relationships. As teachers look for ways to engage students with the technology, they must ask themselves, "What is the problem to which this can be applied?" It may sometimes be a Faustian bargain, because often something important

Figure 5-3. Sailing Through the Crosscurrents of Our Transitional Age

is given and something important is taken away. The quality of the technological content, the connection to important subject matter, and a recognition of the characteristics of effective instruction are central factors in determining instructional success. School is, after all, a place where students should come into contact with caring adults and learn to work together in groups.

Another factor is the human attribute of creating ourselves in the presence of others. The self is in continuous formation. At least some of this search for identity has to take place among others. Autonomous private behavior can inhibit the social nature of literacy development. An impersonal system of media distraction can retard the building of social capacities through genuine human interaction. We have to be sure that the communal aspects of technology-mediated communication grow as group work, conversation, reflection, and critical inquiry begin to take hold. A certain type of interaction can take place online, but some has to be face-to-face so that learners can work together to control the interpretation of what they see and hear.

An Interactive Multimedia Learning Environment

Harmonizing the educational present and the educational future means reinventing the schools, attending to support mechanisms, and having the courage to take the lead on certain issues. Every age seeks out the appropriate medium or combination of media to confront the mysteries of human learning.

Technology gives us a representational medium that can be an animated wonderland, an interactive book, a theatre, a sports arena, and even a potential life form. Along with its associates, the computer provides for the rapid dissemination of ideas and gives us a new stage for participatory experiences.

The next great medium for literacy-generating activities and storytelling is digital. Every effort should be made to help students creatively use and "write" with these new compositional tools. It would be a shame not to put our powerful representational media to the highest tasks of society. Computers and their associates have an immense capacity for creating learning experiences that take us beyond today's games and gimmicks to an interactive experience that probes the important questions of human life.

Having a solid educational agenda is more important than having the latest hardware. New information and communications technologies can be used to help students understand complex issues, solve problems creatively, and apply these solutions to real-life situations. It is bound to be engaging, but it takes effort, planning, and good teachers to make it meaningful. With the high-tech explosion of possibilities, it is important to remember that the curriculum connections must be filtered through the mind of the teacher.

As technological potential and hazard intrude on our schools, there is general agreement that teachers need high-tech inservice training to deal with the explosion of electronic possibility. Knowledgeable teachers are the key to positive change. For technology to reach its potential means making a substantial commitment to helping teachers learn how to use it effectively. Teachers need sustained professional development, common planning time, and opportunities to talk with colleagues. They also need to be encouraged to attend conferences and participate in online teacher networks. By funneling more resources to teachers and classrooms, policy makers can help the schools to develop practices that reflect a technology-intensive era and what is known about effective instruction.

Creating the Future

Once there is a critical mass of teachers regularly using technology and sharing ideas electronically, the highly developed textbook industry will shift to providing more high-tech products. Sitting back and predicting the future of today's digital media is a little like predicting the future of art. We should not be surprised when things turn out different from what we expect. The best approach is to be proactive by actively participating in what is happening. Teachers are better positioned to figure out the needs of their students than are high-tech companies.

As John Schaar has pointed out, the future is not a result of choices among alternative paths offered by the present, but a place that is created—first with the mind and the will, and then with activity. It is not a place we are going to, but one we are creating. As far as the schools are concerned, exploring the relationships among oral, written, visual, and digital modes of communication is bound to be increasingly important to literacy instruction in the age of information. Here there are few models and no road maps. The roads to the future are not found but made, and the activity of making them changes both the maker and the destination.

Media technology is constantly growing in its ability to integrate information and communication in a way that gives instant access to scattered information, multimedia simulation, titillating cyber dramas, and geographically diverse people. This will give teachers powerful tools for teaching subject matter, solving pressing problems, and reaching students. New technological advances beckon us with exciting possibilities for communication, knowledge acquisition, and interactive multimedia learning. The technology has the potential to release rivers of dynamic information that can be directed toward solving specific teaching and learning problems. During the next decade, a digital nervous system of communication and information technology will be able to unite all systems and processes under a common infrastructure.

The formidable forces of technology are pervasive through every realm of human activity. These forces will increasingly shape the dynamics of our personal and educational lives in the 21st century. The technology-based literacies stemming from these changes will reflect a new state of mind and prompt further qualitative transformations in human communication. The technological potential for propelling literacy and learning into an exciting and perilous new era is rapidly coming online. The challenge is making sure that technology is incorporated into formal schooling in a way that enriches the mind, the body, and the soul.

References

Adams, D., & Hamm, M. (1998). *Collaborative inquiry in science, math and technology.* Portsmouth, NH: Heinemann.

Bertram, B. (1997). Literacy technologies: What stance should we take? *Jefferson Literacy Research 27*, 2.

Children Now. (1996). *Children watching television: The role of advertisers.* Oakland, CA: Author.

Dede, C. J. (1985). Assessing the potential of educational information utilities. *Library Hi Tech, 3* (4), 115–119.

Dwyer, D. (1994, April). Apple classrooms of tomorrow: What we've learned. *Educational Leadership 51* (7) 4–10.

Edwards, C., Gandini, L., & Forman, G. (eds.) (1998). *The hundred languages of children: The Reggio Emilia approach to early childhood education.* (2nd ed.). Stamford, CN: Ablex.

Gay, G., & Bennington, T. (Eds.). (1999). *Information technologies in education: Social, moral, epistemological and practice implications.* San Francisco: Jossey-Bass.

Hendon, R. A. (1997). The implications of internet usage for innovative education. Unpublished manuscript.

Hetland, L., & Veenema, S. (Eds.). (1999). *The Project Zero classroom: Views on understanding.* Cambridge, MA: Harvard College.

International Society for Technology in Education. (2000). *National educational technology standards for teachers.* Eugene, OR: Author.

Lewis, P. (1996, July 7). Adventures can find company on the Internet. *The New York Times*, Website, http://www.nytimes.com.

McKibben, B. (1992). *The age of missing information.* New York: Random House.

Moursund, D. G. (1999). *Project-based learning using information technology.* Eugene, OR: International Society for Technology in Education.

National Education Goals Panel. (1994). *The National Education Goals report 1993: Building a nation of learners.* Washington, DC: Author.

National Registrar of Publishing. (1998). *The standard directory of advertisers.* New Providence, NJ: Readel el Sevier.

National Research Council. (1995). *National science education standards.* Washington, D.C: National Academy Press.

Oppenheimer, T. (1997). The computer delusion. *The Atlantic Monthly.* p. 280.

Simonson, M., Smaldino, S., Albright, M., & Zvacek, S. (2000). *Teaching and learning at a distance: Foundations of distance education.* Bellevue, WA/Paramus, NJ: Merrill/Prentice-Hall.

Stoll, C. (1999). *High tech heretic: Why computers don't belong in the classroom and other reflections by a computer contrarian.* New York: Doubleday.

Tapscott. D. (1998). *Group up digital : The rise of the net generation.* New York: McGraw-Hill.

Woronov, T. (1994, September/October). Assistive technology for literacy produces impressive results for the disabled. *The Harvard Education Letter V10* (5) 6–7.

 # The Internet: Changing the Way We Teach and Learn

---

Gradualism, the idea that change must be smooth, slow, and steady is a common cultural bias....The history of life is a series of stable states, punctuated at rare intervals by major events that occur with great rapidity and help establish the next stable era.

—Stephen J. Gould

For two decades, the Internet was the dull and difficult-to-use province of government-financed research centers. In the early days, scientists had to actually program the computer to send a message. By the mid-1990s, a dramatic shift had occurred. Tim Berners-Lee and his associates developed the World Wide Web and opened up a whole new world. Now the Internet has become a powerful associate of fast-moving technological change. It has already altered how we gather information, how we communicate, and how we learn. In 2001, additional domain names (suffixes) started to dot the Internet. Technological refinement and participation continue to proceed at "Internet speed."

Whether the Internet is a true revolution or simply the latest evolutionary advance in communication technology, there is no guarantee that the rapid pace of today's technological change will continue forever. Globalization, the environment, labor protections, a glut of advertisements, and the deep skill divide between the haves and the have-nots are just some of the potential roadblocks to a Web-intensive future. There are many futures waiting out there, but in the next few years the decentralizing power of the Internet's global network will have a much greater impact on our schools and our society.

Educational and social policy choices will affect the willingness of people to accept new Internet technology in the future. As citizens of the information age, students will need multiple technology-intensive literacies to make their way through life. Educators realize this and recognize the fact that one of the essential survival skills for the multimedia age is the ability to navigate the vast electronic terrain made possible by the global networks of networks, the Internet.

Some Practical Possibilities for Using the Internet in the Classroom

Here we outline some practical tools and related Web sites that can help teachers to integrate the Internet into their day-to-day instructional activities. Guidelines are suggested for assessing the quality of information on the Web; protecting student safety when Internet surfing; using a "Web cam" for recording classroom or real-life activities; undertaking selected classroom computer-based activities; and constructing a simple Web page using Netscape Composer.

What difference has the Internet really made in contributing to the learning experience of students? An online publisher and a computer-oriented television broadcaster (Techtv) gathered a panel of 10 top educators, teachers, administrators, and policy makers in the country to express their opinions on the matter and, in addition, asked them to assess the Internet on five specific points. The panel gave the following "grades":

Pace of wiring our school	C
Training of teachers	D+
General effect on student performance	B+
Specific effects on student performance	
English	B+
History	B-
Science	B
Mathematics	C
Social Science	A
Overall contribution to education	B-

There is general agreement that making good use of the Internet can encourage students' engagement in the learning process and change what students believe they are capable of doing. Educational Web sites such as the one sponsored by the CNET Channel provide rich learning and knowledge building opportunities for young students (Figure 6-1). It may also help students to develop the information-processing skills that are so important in the knowledge-based society and economy in which they will grow up. Although students nowadays have far more access than ever to larger volumes of information online, much of the quality of information to which they are exposed is questionable. In fact, one of the biggest challenges with the Internet is finding exactly the kind of information you can use and making sure that the information you find is reliable.

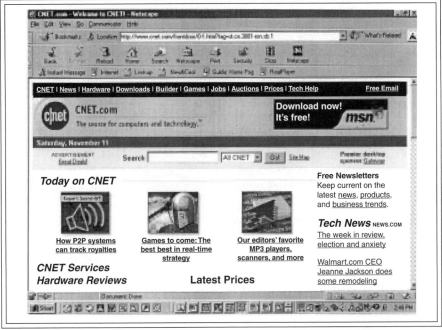

Figure 6-1. The latest technology news in the CNET Channel Web Site.

Positive possibilities are there if students know how to find and use them. For example, the Internet can link students with their peers all over the world, open vast global treasure troves of classroom materials, and help users overcome barriers set up by socioeconomic status, race, and gender. The key to good Internet use in the classroom is putting the educational plan in place first. This requires a pedagogical plan that includes sustained professional development for teachers. The speed at which schools are being wired for the Internet is as fast as the professional development of teachers is slow. The ultimate question of the Internet's educational value cannot be answered independently of the success of teacher preparation and the overall quality of the school system.

Table 6-1 shows what educators think of Internet use in the classroom.

Table 6-1. Reading the Pulse of Educators and Students on the Internet

94%   of teachers and administrators say that computer technology has improved teaching and learning. (1)

76%   of teachers, computer coordinators, and librarians say that the Internet provides students with a serious research tool. (3)

46%   of teachers and administrators cite a small improvement in individualized assessment of student performance due to computers. (1)

29%   of teachers and school superintendents want their district's highest priority to be Internet access. (1)

21%   of teachers use computers for instructional purposes more than three-quarters of the time. (2)

13%   of teachers, computer coordinators, and librarians think that the Internet helps students to achieve better results on standardized tests. (3)

Sources:
(1) Josten's Learning Corp./AASA. 1,001 teachers and school superintendents were surveyed. Margin of error of 3 percentage points. Cited in *USA Today*, 4/11/97.

(2) *USA Today* poll, conducted by CNN and the National Science Foundation. Based on telephone interviews with 744 students in grades 7-12. Margin of error 4 percentage points. Cited in *USA Today*, 4/97.

(3) Market Data Retrieval Survey. Based on random sampling sent to 6,000 teachers, computer coordinators, and school librarians. Cited in *USA Today*, 3/1/97.

Mining the "Gold" From the Electronic Treasure Trove

Schools are finding much to like on the Web and just as many traps to avoid. Just about anyone can publish anything they like on the Internet. Some of it should not be viewed by children. On the technological side, Internet resources often have multiple formats, and sites disappear overnight. Change occurs at an increasingly rapid pace, and information becomes dated even faster. Some schools run the risk of using Internet access just for the sake of using it. Others are caught between fads, ads, and isolated computer labs. The key to success is technologically literate teachers who can balance electronic learning with other classroom activities.

Although most schools now have some kind of Internet connection, it is often unclear how that access is being used to find quality information that can enhance learning.

Searching for information on the Internet is different from traditional paper-based research, due to the peculiarities of the electronic medium. Internet searching is such a common activity now. In their third annual survey of the use of the Internet by schools, Quality Education Data, a market research company that studied 400 K–12 teachers, found that 82% of the schools have an Internet connection. More classrooms are being wired, in addition to libraries or computer laboratories. About 69% of the teachers use the Internet at least once weekly as a teaching aid; about 66% use it to get curriculum material; 46% use it for professional development; and 44% use it for lesson planning. About 49% of the teachers reported that their students use the Internet at least once a week for research purposes.

Guidelines for Evaluating Information on the Internet

Authorship

First, find out who wrote the piece. Is this person well-known or well-regarded in his or her field? If not, depend on other information to establish the value of this author. Does another known expert or author refer to this person? Is this author's Web site linked to a trustworthy source? Does the author give biographical information, including institutional affiliation and appropriate credentials, that can be checked? Is there a telephone number or e-mail address given so that the author can be queried directly?

Body of Work

Take a good look at the body of the work. Is it an abstract, a summary, or the full text? Does the author indicate where this paper was published or presented previously? What is the purpose of the author—to inform, advocate a position, or stimulate discussion?

The Publishing Body or Sponsor

If information on the author is scanty, check the organization that published his or her work. In the world of printed material, peer review usually guarantees the quality of the work. On the Internet, one can be more vigilant in assessing the level of authority of the publisher by doing the following:

- Check to see if the name of the organization is given. Look for it in the header, footer, or distinctive watermark (i.e., a faint graphic design in the background of the document) that indicates the document is part of an official academic or scholarly Web site. If this isn't there, is there a link to such a page? Is there a Webmaster that can be contacted?
- Find out if the publishing organization is renowned in the subject being investigated. What is the relationship between the organization and the author?
- Is this author's work part of the official organizational Web site, or does it reside in his or her personal Internet account? Check out the uniform resource locator (URL) of the author's work.

The Author's Bias or Point of View

The author's organizational affiliation provides clues to his or her possible slant on the subject represented in the work. First, look at the URL of the document in question. Does it reside on the Web server of an organization that may have a stake in the issue being discussed? If the Web site is a corporate one, it may be safely assumed that information concerning the firm will portray it in a highly favorable light. If the work concerns the product or service of the firm, it is either an open or a disguised advertisement. Take special care in detecting an organization's hidden agenda in publicizing certain pieces of information. What may appear as purely educational or informational material may, in fact, have underlying layers of persuasive tones.

The Author's Knowledge of the Subject

The quality of scholarship of the author is indicated by the following items in the publication: bibliography or references; links to reputable sources of information; knowledge of theories, schools of thought, or techniques related to the topic; discussion of the merit of the new theory or approach in discussing the subject, including its benefits and limitations.

The Accuracy or Verifiability of the Work

A thoughtful author will provide an explanation of the research methods used to gather the information embodied in the work, especially in the interest of allowing readers to replicate the study if they are so inclined. Bibliographic information should be complete and accurate. Sources of nonpublished data should also be acknowledged and provided in the work.

The Currency of the Information

Look for indications of the timeliness of the information provided by the author. The document should indicate when the information was gathered and identify dated information. Copyright dates and "date when last updated" are useful clues.

The Information Presented From Search Engine Results

Evaluating information produced by search engines poses unique challenges. The user needs to know how the search engine decides the order in which search results are presented. Some commercial search engines "sell" top space to advertisers who pay them to do so. The technology behind data retrieval for search engines also informs readers of the nature of the information they are bound to find. Computer-performed induction of data downloads information into the search engine server. Selection criteria used in a search are nonevaluative and may occasionally depend on the availability of a particular server. It leaves in a certain number of words from the body of the text and designates it as the "abstract." It usually equates "relevance" of the finding with the number of times certain terms are repeated in the document. It cannot distinguish types of information other than by file extension.

The Information From "Vanity" Web Sites

Digital technology is making publishing such an increasingly inexpensive and speedy venue that resorting to "vanity" publishing has been very tempting for authors. "Vanity" publishing means that authors pay to self-publish and then distribute their own books. Online publishing has decreased the cost and increased the distribution potential. One of the objections to vanity publishing is the lack of collaborative critiquing of one's work called "peer review." This process, which involves the blind analysis of the work by one's professional peers, has ensured "quality control" in the information being presented to the public through publishing houses. Publications resulting from "vanity" presses, whether paper based or online, should be avoided in many cases. Readers should be vigilant about looking into whether or not other experts, editors, or fact checkers in the field have reviewed the work in question.

Distinguishing Hard Information From Disguised Advertising

One of the more difficult things to look out for is "infotainment" disguised as objective information. Business Web sites can package information so cleverly that what is really disguised advertising could read as a factual, expert report. One example of this is the benchmark test results of computer hardware and software. A table or chart depicting statistics on how well or how poorly certain computer hardware or software products performed against their nearest competitors can be very impressive and persuasive. It's always wise to check the organization that undertook the product test and inquire into which organization owns or sponsors the Web site where the study's findings are being disseminated. It should come as no surprise if the manufacturer of the "best" product is also the sponsor or owner of the Web site where the findings are announced.

Table 6-2 features questions that students can ask themselves when evaluating information gathered from the Internet.

Table 6-2. Questions for Evaluating Information on the Internet

Who?

- Who wrote what I am reading?
- Who maintains the Internet site?
- Who would accept this information as authoritative (e.g., my teacher, my friends, my mother?

What?

- What kind of Internet site is it: educational (.edu); busi-

cont.

ness (.com); organization (.org); accredited museums worldwide (.museum); general use (.info); or someone's personal home page?

- What exactly am I reading (e.g., research article, editorial gossip)?
- What information from this Internet source could I include in a bibliographic citation (e.g., footnotes)?

Where?

- Where are the credentials of the author or of the people responsible for the Internet site?
- Where exactly did I find this information, and can I get back there?

When?

- When was this originally written?
- When was the last time this Internet site was updated?
- When I go back to find this Internet site again, will it be there?

Why?

- Why was this originally written?
- Why was this specific information put on the Internet (e.g., general information, to sell a product; to enlisting support.)
- Why was searching the Internet better than using print sources (besides being more fun and taking side trips to irrelevant but interesting Internet sites)?

How?

- How accurate and up to date is the information?
- How well organized and written is the information?
- How can I repeat this search quickly and efficiently if I need this information again?

Source: Multiple sources.

The following are suggested Web site resources for evaluating Web site information:
- The ABC's of Web Site Evaluation
  http://kathyschrock.net/abceval/index.htm
- Evaluating Internet-Based Information: A Goals-Based

cont.

Approach
http://www2.ncsu.edu/unity/lockers/project/meridian/
feat2-6/feat2-6.html
- Evaluating Web Resources
http://muse.widener.edu/Wolfgram-Memorial-Library/
webevaluation/webeval.htm
- WWW CyberGuide Ratings for Content Evaluation
http://www.cyberbee.com/guide1.html
- Evaluation of World Wide Web Sites: An ERIC Digest
http://ericir.syr.edu/ithome/digests/edoir9802.html
- ED's Oasis Evaluation Guidelines
http://www.classroom.com/edsoasis/evaluation.html

Suffixes Added to Reduce ".com" Crowding

The original Internet domains—.com, org., and .net—
adopted in the 1980s have become home for about 40
million Web sites that have used up the most obvious ad-
dresses. The Internet Corporation, a nonprofit organization created at the request of the federal government,
received dozens of proposals for new domain names. They
settled for the following seven new ones. There may be
more domains added in the future.
- .aero: for airports, flight reservations, airlines, and
related industries
- .biz: for businesses
- .coop: for business cooperatives such as credit unions
and rural electric coops
- .info: for general use
- .museum: for accredited museums worldwide
- .name: for individuals
- .pro: for professionals such as doctors and lawyers

Safety on the Internet

The Internet has been both a boon and a bane for students
and educators. Educators and parents have been especially
concerned about protecting children from inappropriate and
unwholesome information and especially from unsavory characters who may be personal threats to children. New Internet

users appear to be more gullible, and their fascination with technology often overshadows the need for sharpening their critical thinking powers. Providing digital highways for the immediate and wide-scale spread of information, or even mis-information and disinformation, the Internet has facilitated the spread of hoaxes, false virus warnings, chain letters, or just plain lies. One casualty of online hoaxes was a man whose name was falsely attached to the online sale of T-shirts with offensive slogans about the Oklahoma City bombing of 1995. An America Online (AOL) subscriber posted Kenneth Zeran's name and telephone number on a bulletin board advertising "Naughty Oklahoma T-Shirts." Kenneth, the innocent victim, eventually received death threats as a result of this and lost a lawsuit he brought against AOL for being the Internet service provider (ISP) for the malicious originator of the messages. The law does not hold ISPs responsible for the nature of the con-tent posted by their customers.

E-commerce sites also seduce children into making unscru-pulous purchases that they are not in a position to make, and this causes financial havoc for their parents.

There have been institutional efforts to block students from access to objectionable information on the Web, but the effects have been unpredictably unpleasant. Students of Jan Shakofsky, a humanities teacher at the Benjamin Cardozo High School in Queens, New York, got the message "access denied" when they tried to research topics such as breast cancer, anor-exia and bulimia, child labor, and AIDs. Even John Steinbeck's *Grapes of Wrath* was blocked out because there is a passage in the book describing a woman who allows a starving man to suckle at her breast. Now teachers are complaining that similar information-filtering efforts by the certain local Boards of Edu-cation—using products such as I-Gear made by Urlabs, a sub-sidiary of Symantec—are hampering the research efforts of students and making them less competitive than their counter-parts in other areas of the country. Although much more nar-rowly defined information-filtering efforts allowing specification of blocked information may be promoted, locating one's school between absolutely free information access and discretionary selection of information that students may tap into requires a delicate balancing act.

Table 6-3 lists some guidelines for parents and teachers to share with children before they surf the net.

Table 6-3. Net Guide for Children

- Do not give out your full name, password, address, phone number, or credit card number.
- Do not share with just anyone online information such as the names of your town, school, teachers, friends, Little League or school teams, camps, or clubs.
- Consult a parent or teacher before giving out any kind of personal information asked for by the Web site.
- If you don't know what to do about disturbing information you see on the Net, consult your parents or teachers.
- Inform your parents and teachers about new online friends that you've made. Have them check out these new friends before you start communicating via e-mail or instant messages.
- Do not meet with friends you make online until you let your parents or teachers know about this meeting; have them come along.
- Be polite and act civil. Do not insult, offend, pick a fight, or say something unpleasant to someone in an online discussion, a chat room session, or an e-mail message.
- Consult your parents or teachers if you are being asked strange questions on a Web site.
- Don't answer e-mail messages from strangers and don't open attachments these messages contain.
- Be careful what you say in e-mail messages—these can be saved and stored and used against you in the future.
- If someone is harassing you online, for example, in a chat room or through instant messaging, report this person to your parents or teachers. They could report this person to your Internet service provider and even have this person blocked from contacting you.
- If you want to buy something online and you do not have a credit card of your own, ask your parent's permission first before proceeding to the checkout.
- Visit only good and useful Web sites, as your parents or teachers can access sites you've recently visited.
- Learn about how to use virus protection software so that you do not transfer viruses to your personal computer at home or at school.
- If you receive a chain letter online, delete the message immediately.

cont.

- Search for information to verify the message of a suspected hoax.
- Go directly to the home pages or Web sites of organizations that are the subject of Internet rumors. Better yet, you can e-mail the Web master of a particular organization, who can help to forward your questions to the right parties in the organization.

Source:
Adapted from "Net Guide for Kids," November 1999, http://familypc.zdnet.com/safety/security/feature/2942/. Including ideas from: "Yahooligans Rules for Online Safety" at: http://www.yahooligans.com/docs safety/.

Creating Lively Classroom Material Using a Web Cam

Spice up classes with lively and wacky video shows that students can produce using "Net cams" or "Web cams." This newest kid on the technological block" is a device that lets the user create original movies, record moving pictures to send as "V-mail" (i.e., "video mail") over the Internet, and hold live video conferencing sessions with other persons, also over the Web. An extremely helpful and resource-rich Web site is that of the Vulcan Ventures and its cable channel, Techtv. This television channel and Web site (www.techtv.com) posts the latest information and tips on using electronic toys and tools. Table 6-4 explains fundamental Web-camming principles to help the user understand this particular technology better. Table 6-5 gives guidelines on how to assemble the hardware and software pieces before embarking on a real project. At this point, it would be good to review chapter 2, especially the concepts of storyboarding and assembling a video production.

Table 6-4. Basic Web Camming Principles

1. Use image files of the highest quality at the smallest possible file size. These are usually larger, minimally compressed images. You certainly want your pictures to look very good without taking up too much computer drive space. Avoid the Progressive JPEG file for-

cont.

mat for pictures. Although this format loads into the Web browser faster, the image itself can look "blocky" while it is downloading itself, and a number of Web browsers are not equipped to display this type of file format.

2. Choose the appropriate image file format for your picture or movie depending on your computer system's operating system and how you plan to use the files: JPEG, GIF, Bitmap, PICT, AVI, QuickTime, or MPEG.

3. Choose the appropriate sound file format from among the following: AU (Audio Unix); AIFF (Audio Information File Format); WAV (WAVeform); Macintosh System Sound; MIDI (Musical Instrument Digital Interface); QuickTime; AVI (Audio Video Interleaved); MPEG (Motion Pictures Expert Group); and as of late, MP3. The two formats recommended for sound effects, voice recordings, and music clips are WAV and AU files. MIDI files are best for movie background music and for your Web pages.

4. In Web camming, the standard three choices for image size are full screen (640 X 480 pixels), half screen (320 X 240 pixels), and quarter screen (160 X 120 pixels). The last two choices are popular for Web camming. Once again, the larger the screen size, the more memory is required.

5. Choose an appropriate color depth option or the number of possible colors for a particular image. The higher the color depth, the better the color quality at the cost of memory, once again. The standard choices are 256 grays (8-bit color), 256 colors (8-bit color), thousands of colors (16-bit color), and millions of colors (24-bit color).

6. Adjust the level of light of the image you're working with. Software products like QuickCam have sliders that allow you to increase brightness or contrast in either direction. Some products also let you adjust the white level or black level. When you lower the white level, you avoid the problem of "blooming," which happens when white light shines all over the picture too brightly.

7. Adjust the hue and saturation levels of the image, referring to the elements of color and intensity of color. Software products provide sliders that will let you adjust the hue and saturation settings. Increasing the

cont.

red tones gives the images a warm look, and increasing the blue tones give them a cooler look. Higher saturation levels make the images look intense, and lower saturation levels tone the colors down.

8. Choose an appropriate frame rate for your cam. The frame rate determines the number of images or frames captured per second. Acceptable quality comes with a frame rate of 30 frames per second. Faster frame rates take up larger file sizes, but the reproduction quality is smoother. Lower frame rates take up smaller file sizes, but the resulting image is choppy.

9. When file size is an issue, you can resort to file compression tools. The process of compression makes the file seemingly smaller. The higher the compression factor, the poorer the quality of the image. There are also different compression options. The standard ones are Intel Indeo and Radius Cinepak. Avoid using proprietary compression schemes or techniques that are unique to a particular brand of hardware or software. They may make it hard for you to share your files with friends or classmates.

10. You may choose the overall audio level for the Macintosh by selecting one among five options: phone quality, speech quality, radio quality, music quality, and CD quality.

**Table 6-5. Setting Up Web Cam
Hardware and Software**

Preparing the Web Cam Hardware

1. When you unpack your Web cam box, you should find the cam, a cable, a manual, and a CD-ROM or floppy disk for the cam software. If you already have a handheld video camera, you may use this instead. It usually delivers better image quality and adjusts better to bright light and darkness.

2. The Web cam may be shaped like a small ball (e.g., Logitech's QuickCam), or an egg (e.g., VideoBlaster Web Cam II), or a conventional camera (e.g., ARS Innovations' Compro Dcam). See Figure 6-2 for a picture of the Quick Cam Pro 3000. You may put the cam on top

cont.

of your computer monitor or anywhere else where you would like to mount it in order to get the images you want to capture.

3. Your Web cam connects to your computer through any of the following: parallel port (Windows), your printer or modem serial port (Macintosh), or a Universal Serial Bus (USB) port (Windows 95, 98 or Macintosh System 8.5).

4. It's a good idea to get a video capture card so that you can go beyond the limitations of Web cams. Also, few computers have built-in video capture. This card will allow you to plug your Web cam or video camera into your computer. Some of these cards may be plugged into a PowerMac, a G3, or a Pentium system's PCI slot. A video-capable Macintosh system usually offers two sets of video-in ports: the standard RCA ports and the S-Video (Super VHS) ports. Many video cameras use standard RCA cables.

5. For sound effects, you'll need a microphone, a pair of speakers, and a sound card. You'll also need software for recording and playing sounds. For the Macintosh, Simple Sound is recommended.

Working With the Web Cam Software

The following are the steps to take in making your initial video production. Since most schools use Macintosh computers, this short tutorial will feature SiteCam for the Macintosh. (Check out Rearden Technology at http://www.rearden.com for more product details.)

1. Install the SiteCam package from Rearden Technology on your Macintosh computer.

2. Select "New" from SiteCam's file menu to create a new file. Then, select "File/Save" and assign a file name to your new file. SiteCam thereafter creates JPEG files automatically.

3. Preview a picture by selecting "Document/Preview" to enable SiteCam to display a demographic.

4. Change the frame rate for your video preview. Do this by selecting "Document/Video Refresh." The Settings dialog box will appear with Video Refresh options. SiteCam measures the frame rate in "ticks" rather than frames per second. The default setting is 45 ticks or one frame per $3/4$ of a second. If you want a faster frame rate, enter a low number. Conversely, if you want a slower frame rate to put less of a strain on the Macintosh, en-

cont.

ter a high number. Click the Save button.

5. Adjust the brightness and contrast levels using the Video Refresh dialog box. When this box is opened, click the Refresh Rate (1-255) checkbox. Type a number in the box to the right of this window to tell SiteCam how often you want to change the settings. A low number as opposed to a high number will result in refreshing the brightness/contrast much more often. Another way of doing this is to select "File/Configure Digitizer." From the dialog box, select "Image" from the list box and make changes according to what you see in the Preview Area. Click OK when you're done.

6. Adjust the picture size and color depth by choosing "File/Settings" and then choosing "Output Format" from the Setup list. In the Video Capture Size list, you may select 50% for a 320 X 240 picture or 25% for a smaller size of 160 X 120. Choose an appropriate color depth from the Colors list. Save your work.

7. Adjust the image quality by choosing "Document/Output Format." When a settings dialog box appears, select an option from the Image Quality list and click OK.

8. Determine when SiteCam should update your pictures by selecting "Document/Interval" to show the SiteCam Settings dialog box with the Interval options. Select the "Save Picture/Movie Every" option to indicate to SiteCam just how often you would like it to save your pictures. In the list that you will see, select a number and then, a unit of time (seconds, minutes, hours). You may also run your Web cam only during certain hours. Click the "Only" box in the "Active" section of the window and choose numbers from the pull-down lists for starting and ending times and for a.m. or p.m. You may also want to run the Web cam only on certain days of the week.

9. You may "timestamp" (date and time) your image files so the viewers may know when the current pictures were taken. Select "Document/Caption 1" from the document menu. Choose a date and time format in the Timestamp section of the Caption Setup dialog box. Also pick the appropriate font, size, and style from the given list. In addition, you may choose text and background colors and horizontal and vertical positions for where the timestamp information will appear. Save your settings.

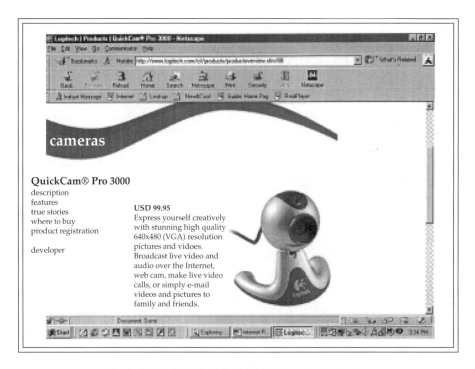

Figure 6-2. The Quick Cam Pro 3000 Model by Logitech.

Practical Internet Classroom Activities

Children can be eased into full engagement in the use of computers using the following fun-filled activities:

Personalizing Your Sports Cards

Materials. MGI Photo Suite (Windows CD, MGI Software 888-644-7638) or any home publishing or word processing software that lets the user input images or scan photos. For students who love trading sports cards, this activity will absolutely be a treat.

1. Create a digital file of the photo. There are different ways of coming up with a digital file of a photograph. One may use a digital camera, scanner, or commercial scanning services to produce this file.

2. Select a photo. Launch MGI PhotoSuite and select "Create a Sports Card" from the MGI Activity Guide. Select an image file

to display on the front side of the card using the dialog box that appears.

3. Resize the image. The user may adjust the size of the image by clicking on one of the handles that appear around the image once it loads. While holding the mouse button down, shrink or stretch the graphic image at the handles until the right size is reached. The image that appears on the template will be the image that prints. After making the image fit, use the mouse to center it on the card template.

4. Print the picture. Click on the printer button to print the image of the front side of the card on high-quality paper.

5. Creating the back of the sports card. Click on "Fun" on the taskbar and scroll down to Sports Card Info. Blank areas will appear for such bits of information as name, hometown, position, team, league, and coach. Fill in the blanks and then print this side of the card.

6. Making it stick. Use scissors to trim the sides of both the front and back sides of the sports card. PhotoSuite provides card stock, cut to size, with an adhesive surface on both sides. Peel back the covering of one side of the card stock, carefully align one of the printouts, and affix it to the sticky side. Do this for both sides of the card.

This activity was adapted from Sam Mead, "Make Personalized Sports Cards," Family PC, www.familypc.zdnet.com. There has been a change: www.zdnet.com is now www.techtv.com.

Making Airplanes

Materials. Print Artist Craft Factory (Windows 95 CD, Sierra On-Line, 800-757-7707), scissors, and color printer.

This activity will appeal to would-be pilots in the bunch. While the instructions here are specific to building a small airplane, the software package may be used for creating other things like mobiles, puppets, and board games.

1. Select the airplane project. Choose "Airplane" at the Craft Factory Main Menu and "Just for Fun" from the Category Box. Choose "Jet Fighter" from the templates and drag the image to the workspace. We will tweak the image a little bit to suit our fancy.

2. Personalize the airplane. The template has an area for entering a personalized message. In the "Text Grabber," type the name of the airplane—for instance, "Great Spirit"—and drag it to the work space. Adjust the size of the text area by dragging the box arrows and using the rotating handle to place it in the right spot on the template. Be sure to position the text so that it reads the same way on each side so the message can be seen when the plane is folded.

3. Customize the plane. Delete the bottom circles of the template after clicking on them. Select the "Graphics Grabber or Basic Shapes" and select a graphical image. Try the "Swirl" design. Drag this design to the template and adjust its size so that it fits between the dotted fold lines, or else it won't show when the airplane is folded. Place it in the example circle; select "Stamp" to duplicate it for the other side, and then drag it into place.

4. Print, fold, and fly the plane. After printing the airplane template, follow the folding instructions and get the plane ready for flight.

This activity was adapted from Michelle Megna, "Personalized Paper Airplanes," Family PC, www.familypc.zdnet.com. There has been a change: www.zdnet.com is now www.techtv.com.

Creating Gift Tags

Materials. Avery Personal Creations Special Occasion Variety Pack #3250, Avery 800-462-8379) Favorite clip art or photographic images (suggested: Broderbund's Print Shop 6.0), and an inkjet printer. This is a great activity for children prior to important gift-giving occasions. They can add that special personal touch using some very easy techniques.

1. Select a template. Select "Greeting Cards" in the Main Print Shop menu. Click "Start from Scratch" on the next screen. A list of greeting card formats will be presented on the following screen. Pick "Avery Mini-Folded Card #3264—Wide" and then click OK.

2. Decorate the card. A blank template of a greeting card will appear. Click on the "Insert Graphic" on the toolbar to add a clip-art image or fancy border. The graphic image may be resized by placing the cursor over one of the small black tabs on the edge of the image. Drag these tabs to get the desired size of the image.

3. Make a front-side card headline. Click the "Insert Head-

line" button to put a headline on the front side of the gift tag. Customize the headline by selecting one of the ready-made styles and then click on "Customize," which lets the user play with fancy text distortions and drop shadows.

4. Write a personal message inside the tag. Click on the folded card icon at the bottom of the editing window. Add a graphic image to the inside portion of the tag following the same steps in number 2. Then click on the "Insert Text Block" button to type in a personalized message. Edit the text by double clicking on the box to choose font size, styles, and layout using the buttons on the toolbar. Change the properties of the text box by clicking on the box itself until the black tabs appear. Right click the inside of the box to add background color, a border, and special effects.

5. Save and print the tag. Save the work from the file menu. Put a piece of folded card stock into the printer and choose print from the file menu. After printing this side, flip the page over and turn it end-over-end. Reinsert the folded card stock into the print tray and click OK to print the inside of the tag. Cut the card on the perforation lines, fold it over, and then tape it on top of the gift.

This activity was adapted from Bonnie Georgia, "Great Gift Tags," Family PC, www.familypc.zdnet.com. There has been a change: www.zdnet.com is now www.techtv.com.

Creating Eerie Halloween Masks

Materials. A graphics program (suggested: Microsoft's PictureIt: 800-426-9400), a digital image, heavy-stock paper, rubber bands, scissors, and an inkjet printer. Children will love this activity in preparation for Halloween trick-or-treating. They are not likely to run into classmates or playmates who have an identical mask.

1. Decide on a character to create. To make a digital image of a character, search online for the character—Batman, Superman, Casper the Friendly Ghost, and so forth. Right click the image and then save the image on the computer. Images can also be bought from CD-ROMs or scanned from a book or magazine. To create something different and original, use a graphics program like Microsoft Paint to put a drawing together.

2. Resize the image. The image will need to be resized around

the face. Using Microsoft's PictureIt, open the image, choose "Size & Position/Crop" from the options on the left screen. Doing this will create a square border in the middle of the full image. (PictureIt offers several other shapes for the border, such as a circle or star.) Change the size of the borders by clicking and dragging the green dots located on the sides and corners. Once the character's face is on the borders, click "Done." The face is now the entire image.

3. Refine the image. Enlarging an image makes it somewhat fuzzy. It may have to be refined to give it a sharper look on the screen after it has been enlarged. To sharpen the black lines, select "Special Effects/Blur" or "Sharpen Focus." Move the focus bar to sharpen the image and then click "Done." To lighten up the overall color, choose "Paint & Color Effects/Brightness & Contrast." Use the wheel to adjust the settings. The image will change as the wheel is moved. After the image reaches a satisfactory point, click on "Done" and save the work.

4. Give the image the right size. PictureIt has print features for several sizing options, including "Fit to Page," which is best for full-size face masks. The printed result will fill a letter-size page.

5. Give the mask its finishing touches. Trim the edges around the character's face, cut eye holes in the mask, and attach a rubber band from the back of one ear to the other. Add a T-shirt, shorts, and skateboard to finish the costume. Now, be ready to trick or treat!!

This activity was adapted from Ellen De Pasquale, "Homemade Halloween Masks," Familypc, www.familypc.zdnet.com. There has been a change: www.zdnet.com is now www.techtv.com.

Ordering a Personalized Mouse Pad

Materials. Internet access, custom photo Web site such as www.pix.com. This activity lets students order a personalized version of a mouse pad for their daily use. All they will need is Internet access to a shop such as the www.pix.com Web store.

1. Go to www.pix.com. On the home page of this site, you'll find the department's pull-down menu on the left side. Click on

"All Gifts" and then scroll through the menu of available gift items and choose "Mouse Pad."

2. Pick the "picture basket". Choose "Personalize This Gift" when the mouse pad gift page opens. Click the picture frame icon to select a picture. The next page will show all available images in the Picture Basket. The basket will be empty if the student has not used www.pix.com.

3. Select the picture of choice. Click "Add From My Computer" to add a picture to the basket. Browse the hard drive and choose an image after following the instructions on the next page. Click continue to select the image you want. The image will automatically upload to the Picture Basket. Do this many times over, depending on the number of images desired. After the images are uploaded, the Picture Basket page opens to show a smaller version of the images selected. Click on the specific image to use for the mouse pad.

4. Place the order. After choosing the mouse pad design, indicate the number of items ordered. Proceed to the checkout area and fill in the form you will see with your credit card information and shipping address.

This activity was adapted from "Create a Personalized Mouse Pad" by Bonnie Georgia, Familypc Section, www.familypc. zdnet .com. There has been a change: www.zdnet. com is now www. techtv.com.

The next three activities for the language arts were adapted from selected items in Sheryl Burgstahler and Laurie Utterback's New Kids on The Net: Internet Activities in Elementary Language Arts, Allyn & Bacon, 2000.

Expository Writing: Courageous Kids

This activity will help children to improve their expository writing skills. We will access ZuZu, an online magazine for kids that promotes the sharing of ideas and artwork, specifically related to making the world a better place in which to live.

Materials. Internet access, pen, and paper.

1. Access the ZuZu home page. Using any browser program, go to http://www.zuzu.org/.

2. Choose a story of interest. Ask the students to point at the "Courageous Kids" link, click on it, and select a story that looks interesting.

3. Tell the students to write down your observations. What is the title of the story? Why did you choose it? How does it relate to your life? What is its main message?

4. Have the students write an original story. What story would you write to feature the qualities of courage and integrity that you would like to develop in yourself and others?

5. Then, have them send in their contribution. Scroll to the bottom of the page and type the story in the electronic form. When you are done typing, click the button that says "Click Here to Send us Your Story!"

Activity 7 Writing a Letter of Concern

Children can be challenged to improve their letter writing skills by performing this activity. Take them to the Web site of Care Quest, a letter writing project from kids to sick and injured children.

Materials. Internet access, pen, and paper.

1. Access the Web wite of Care Quest. Use any browser in the computer and type in the following address: http://www.worldkids.net/CareQuest/.

2. Select "Instruction & Info." In this area of the page, have the student select "I would love to write a letter, but am not sure what to say." This link shows suggestions on what to write and even an example of a nice letter. Ask the student to think about the following possible things to write:

- What do you think children who are sick miss the most when they are sick?
- What are different ways you could take care of yourself while you're healthy?
- What are things we could be thankful for while we're healthy?
- What does being sick teach us about ourselves? others?
- What are small things we could do to help ourselves back to health?

- Imagine nice messages you could give to a child to help him or her feel better. What could these messages be?

3. After writing something down, select "For Kids" and then click on "Write Your Letter." An electronic form will pop up within which to write a letter.

4. The letter can also be sent out on traditional paper along with a card to a particular sick child. In that case, select "Special Delivery"—this page will give an address of a child to send a letter to via the Post Office.

Describe a Natural Habitat Using Creative Writing

Children can explore natural wildlife in their minds and express it in colorful writing. For this activity, visit the World Wildlife Fund (WWF) Global Network Web site for access to different types of natural climates.

Materials. Internet access, pen, and paper

1. Access the (WWF) Global Network Web site at http://www. panda.org.

2. When on that site, click the "Just for Kids" link and select "Virtual Wildlife."

3. Select "Wild Places," which will then bring up a drawing of the globe with different climates indicated. With the mouse, select one climate by moving the rectangle over a particular area. This will produce a description of the climate and its characteristics.

4. Imagine visiting this area for the first time. Given the information on the characteristics of this climate, write a scenario about what the area might look like, the types of plants and flowers it might have, the animals that roam around, the temperature, the sounds, the people's clothing.

Create a Simple Web Site

One of the more exciting projects that teachers and students can do together is to create web sites for just about any purpose. One of the better tools to use is Netscape Composer, which is the Web site creation tool built into the browser Netscape Communicator. Its latest version, as of this writing, is 4.76. Please see Figure 6-3 for a picture of the Web site that will be constructed here.

Download a free copy of Netscape Communicator 4.76 by going to http://www.netscape.com. on the Netscape's home page, look at the icon on the upper leftmost corner of the screen, which says, "Download." Click that link and a series of windows will open instructing how to download the latest version of Communicator. Follow those instructions closely. Even when the file has been downloaded, the program is still not installed and usable. After the file is downloaded to the computer's hardrive, execute the installation instructions given by Netscape on the download page just visited.

Figure 6-3. "My Favorite Computer Technology Websites"
project for children using Netscape Composer.

Once Netscape Communicator is installed, click on "Communicator" on the horizontal menu bar. When the vertical menu appears, choose "Composer." This will activate that module in Communicator; once the software is open, follow these instructions to begin to build a Web site.

The following Web page features a certain child's favorite computer technology links. It is an appropriate subject as students learn more and more about computer technology.

1. Click FILE and then choose NEW, BLANK PAGE. This will give a new Netscape page.

2. The cursor will be on the first line, left side of the screen.

Click FORMAT on the horizontal menu and go down to ALIGN and choose CENTER. Just below the icon toolbar, click the down arrow indicating font type and choose "Arial Rounded MT Bold" (or any other font type). For font size (the window next to it), choose 24. Type the following at the top line: "My Favorite Computer Technology Web Sites."

3. Add a horizontal line below the heading. From the Composer toolbar, click the Insert Horizontal Line button (the next-to-the-last button). Or click INSERT on the horizontal menu and choose HORIZONTAL LINE. Composer automatically inserts a horizontal line at the insertion point and adds a space above and below the line. The default horizontal line is four pixels thick, runs the full width of the browser window, and is shaded to create an embossed effect. (The appearance of the line can be altered later by changing the settings in the Horizontal Line Properties dialog box.) Press ENTER three times after the line.

4. Continue to use the same type font, but this time adjust the font size to 12. Also click the icon showing the letter "A" in a slanted fashion to indicate the italic font style. Type the following:

> These are the Web sites I'd like to share with my friends, who may be preschool to age 14. These sites are special to me because they have been preselected by some very important people at the Children and Technology Committee of the Association for Library Service to Children.

Press ENTER three times again.

5. Change the font size to 14 and the font to "Century Gothic" (or choose any other font) before typing the following (still using the same font):

> Computer technology is a kid's important play tool as well. It's good to start early in becoming friends with technology because computers are "cool"—they do all sorts of important work for you and me. They can help us save time and money in preparing documents. Computers allow us to communicate more with our family and friends. Computers—particularly the Internet—keep us in touch with other people who can help us and also learn from us

After typing this, select the third to the last line in this block of text by dragging the pointer across the lines. Click FORMAT on the horizontal menu, select LIST, and then choose BULLETED. This action will produce a bulleted list using the default small black circle bullet style. (There are other bullet styles, but that is something to experiment with later.) Press ENTER three times. Insert a horizontal line.

6. Insert a table on this page. Click the table button in the Composer toolbar. The New Table properties dialog box will be displayed. Type 7 in the Number of rows text box and 2 in the Number of columns text box. Click Center in the Table Alignment area. Type 0 in the Border line width box. Type 90 in the Table width text box. Then, click the OK button. Composer will add the table to the Web page. You'll see dotted lines on the Composer screen—the table will look different when viewed through Netscape Navigator later on. (For now, type the given values for the table. Study what the table attributes mean later by accessing the Netscape Composer online help guide. For now, just produce the table.)

Type the following table headings: "Fabulous Web Sites" (using Arial Rounded MT bold font type or any other font type, 12 points, italicized) in the left cell, first row, and "What the Web Site is About" in the right cell, first row. Then, type the following information in the table, taken from http://www.ala.org/parentspage/greatsites/science.html#e.

Use Century Gothic font type or any other font , size 12 points, for the contents of the table. Type "Children's Software" in the left column, second row. Then, type "This site is for information on computer books and software to help children learn about computers, programming, and creating multimedia programs" in the right column, second row. Do the same for the following other entries:

Computer History and Development — This is a useful site for detailed information on computer background projects. Includes links to the abacus through supermarket scanners.

Electronic Origami Shop — This site has wonderful kaleidescope pictures, puzzles, and online art sponsored by IBM; it includes a history of "Big Blue."

Finding Data on the Internet — You've cast your nets into an ocean of information, but still aren't finding what you need? That's what happens when you're not using the right tools to mine the Internet. This site has very good tools you can use to improve your searches.

Discovery School — In the "Student" channel of this web site, a different scientist is featured in the "Scientists at Work" section of the "Science Fair Central." this is a great place for you to meet inspiring scientists who use computer technology in their work. for instance, there is Ronald Kriz, Director of the CAVE automatic Virtual Environment Facility at Virginia Tech. In this lab, he uses supercomputers to create a virtual reality theater to visualize scientific problems.

The Tech Museum of Innovation — Find out more about computers, satellites, DNA, robots, lasers, and other "neat" stuff. This is an educational resource to engage all kinds of people in experiencing technologies that affect their lives and is meant to inspire the young to become inventors of the future.

7. Next we will embed hyperlinks to the computer technology Web sites that are featured in the table. Figure 6-4 shows the Web site of the Discovery Channel's virtual "School." Let's start with Children's Software. Select this text. Right click the selected text and then point to "Create Link Using Selected" on the pop-up menu. Type http://www.kidsdomain.com in the link to the area, just below the phrase "Link to a page location or local file:" and then click the OK button. Repeat these steps for the following:

Computer History and Development
http://www.digitalcentury.com/encyclo/update/comp_hd.html

Electronic Origami Shop
http://www.ibm.com/stretch/EOS

Finding Data on the Internet
http://www.robertniles.com/data

Discovery School
http://www.discoveryschool.com

The Tech Museum of Innovation
http://www.thetech.org

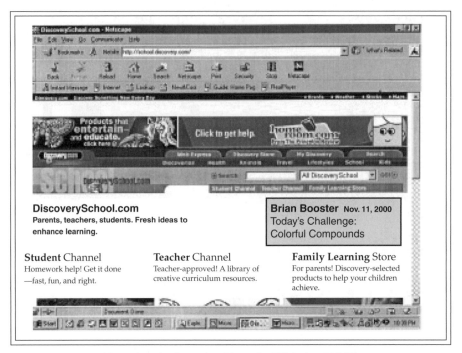

Figure 6.4. The "Invention Dimension" Web site of M.I.T.
is one of the favorite links in this Web page.

8. We are now ready to add graphical images to this Web page. First, it is necessary to have graphical files available on the disk drive so that these files can be "fetched" by Composer. Graphic files contain images or pictures and may be using either of the two most popular graphic file extensions, GIF or JPEG. To find graphic files on the Web, use any search engine, type in the suggested search phrase "animated GIF files," and then look through the results and find an animated GIF (graphics interchange format). Focus the cursor on the image, click the right mouse button and choose Save Image As and save the file either on the A Drive or D Drive (Temp Folder). A file name will usually be provided, or another name can be chosen (this will help later if many graphic files are stored on the disk).

9. To add graphical images to the Web page, click Insert in Composer's horizontal menu and when the Image Properties Window pops up, make sure the Image Tab is selected. Click the Choose File button in order to import the image drive from the appropriate drive. Click on the file name of the image and then press Open and OK.

10. An image cannot be positioned at any random location on the page. It must be located in reference to surrounding text. Thus, the image may be embedded in the beginning, middle, or

end of the paragraph, or in a paragraph of its own. Click a button in the Text Alignment or Wrapping Around Images area to specify how the image will be aligned on the Web page and the manner in which text will wrap around it. There are seven buttons in this area, from left to right:

TEXTTOP — Aligns top of the image with the top of text.

ABSCENTER — Aligns the vertical center of the image with the vertical center of text.

CENTER — Aligns center of image with baseline of text.

BOTTOM — Aligns bottom of image with baseline of text (default setting).

ABSBOTTOM — Aligns bottom of image with bottom of descenders (i.e., tails of letters such as g and y that extend below baseline).

LEFT — Aligns image with left margin and wraps text around its right side.

RIGHT — Aligns image with right margin and wraps text around its left side.

11. The size of the image can be altered in two ways. First, enter values in the Height and Width windows under "Dimensions" in the Image tab. Perhaps an easier way would be to manually size an image after placing it on the page by clicking one of its edges and dragging it to the appropriate size. Specify the amount of white space between the edge of the image and the closest text by filling in values in the "Space around image" area, which asks the number of pixels in the Left and Right, Top and Bottom, and Solid Border.

12. To add sound: Download the sound file on the appropriate drive—most likely the floppy A drive. Turn on the speakers. The download procedure for sound files is identical to the one for graphical files: right click the mouse and find the option for saving the file, which would be Save Link As.

13. Select the text or image for the hyperlink anchor. Click the Link icon on the toolbar or choose the Insert button on the horizontal menu and then click Link. Depending on whether the hyperlink anchor is text or an image, the Image Properties or Character Properties dialog box will open.

From the Properties dialog box, choose the Link tab. Go to the Link to Text box and enter the filename of the sound file. Better yet, use the Choose File button and browse for the file in the Link to File dialog box. By default, only HTML files may be displayed. Click on the drop down arrow to view the common sound file formats from the Files of Type window and choose the file name. Sound files will have the following formats:

AU — This is one of the more common sound formats and has the .au filename extension. AU sound files have an 8-bit sample resolution, a sampling rate of 8 Khz, and are recorded in mono.

WAVE — This is used in Windows-based systems; uses the .WAV extension; recorded in 8-bit or 16-bit sample resolutions, mono or stereo; has a wide range of sampling rates; uses different compression schemes.

RealAudio — Used for real-time sound retrieval over low to high bandwidth connections. Sound quality is not as good as AU or WAVE files even though its files are smaller.

AIFF/AIFC — Audio Interchange File Format developed by Apple for the Macintosh operating system; has an .aiff or .aif filename extension; either an 8-bit or 16-bit sound file, mono or stereo, with different sampling rates.

SND — Used for the Macintosh operating system; not widely used.

MPEG — Moving Pictures Expert Group; format used mainly for video clips; has good compression capability.

After selecting the name for the sound file, click OK to close the Properties dialog box. Save the homepage file. Preview the page on Netscape Navigator. Test the link and play the sound file.

14. To add video: Download video files on the appropriate drive—most likely the A drive. If the file is extremely large, use the C or D drive (Temp folder).

15. Select the text or image for the hyperlink anchor. Click the Link icon on the toolbar or choose the Insert button on the horizontal menu and then click Link. Depending on whether the hyperlink anchor is text or an image, the Image Properties or Character Properties dialog box will open. From the Properties dialog box, choose the Link tab. Go to the Link To Text box and enter the file name of the video file. Better yet, use the Choose File button and browse for the file in the Link to File dialog box. By default, only HTML files may be displayed. Click on the drop down arrow to view the common video file formats from the Files of Type window and choose a file name. The more common video file formats are as follows:

AVI — Windows supports this standard video format, also known as Video for Windows (VfW); uses the .avi extension in the filename; not widely supported by other operating systems.

MPEG — Moving Pictures Expert Group; uses the .mpeg filename extension; compresses files well but decompression can take time; some MPEG formats may require an MPEG board to be installed on the computer system; MPEG players are available for all operating systems.

QuickTime — Developed for Macintosh systems; uses .qt or .mov filename extensions; QuickTime players are available for all operating systems; ideal format for cross-platform support.

16. After selecting the name for the video file, click OK to close the Properties dialog box. Save the home page file.

17. Preview the page on Netscape Navigator. Test the link and play the video file.

18. Add an e-mail address. Select a text or image to become the anchor for the e-mail hyperlink. From the INSERT menu, choose Link or click the Insert Link button on the toolbar. This will open the Character Properties dialog box (or, in the case of an image, the Image Properties dialog box) with the Link tab displayed. The selected text or the filename of the selected image will appear in the Link Source box. In the Link To text box, type mailto:, followed by the e-mail address (e.g., mailto:name @domain.com). Click OK to close the dialog box and insert the link into the Web page. A visitor who clicks on the link can go to the e-mail program instead of another Web page.

19. Change the background color of Web page. Click on FORMAT on horizontal menu and go down to Page Colors and Properties. Click the box beside Background — a color pallette will automatically appear. Choose a color and click OK. It will be applied to the entire Web page.

20. Change the color of text fonts. Select the text to which to add color. Click Format on the horizontal menu bar, choose Color. A color pallette will automatically appear. Click on a color from the pallette that automatically appears. Make font color changes to any part of the document.

If we lay the right groundwork, we will find new ways of using and interacting on the Web. Video as Input (V.A.I.) is just the latest twist. After being downloaded from the Web it allows us to take part in high-immersion, interactive simulations without the gawky gloves and headsets of late '90s virtual reality. A video camera on or in the computer places an image in the visual narrative, and the whole scene responds to the user's body movements. The day will come when this can be done online by live and simulated participants from around the world. Whatever the specifics, as the Web becomes something more than a two-dimensional tool for research and communication, it can powerfully influence new ways of thinking, collaborating, and learning.

Shaping the Use of Technology in the Schools

The future is more than the past with a twist. The first-generation Internet was a commercial-free public space. The second generation has become heavily saturated with advertisements and every odd voice out there. Although the ads and cranks may be here to stay, the Web is becoming a faster and more visually intensive global network that will soon connect a billion computers, Web appliances, cell phones, and handheld devices like the Palm Pilot. Beyond these trends there are as many possible futures for the Internet as there were for broadcast television 50 years ago. More total convergence with other media is one possibility; another is to keep a little separation and let each medium or combination compete for viewers' time and attention. Understanding how to tap into the Internet's vast resources to enhance learning is more important than which hardware is used to open the door.

Putting the human factor first remains the key to making the best use of technology. For the Internet to reach its full educational potential will require the active participation of educators, policy makers, computer manufacturers, and software developers. The global system that is evolving will require much more than simply adding more computers, wireless technologies, and Web TV boxes. Digital devices are becoming more able to interact with each other, and they are interacting with the network in unpredictable ways—a little like a biological organism.

The capabilities of computers, communication devices, digital texts, artificial intelligence, Internet applications, and communication devices continue to expand. In connecting teaching and learning to Web resources, things are changing so fast and the diffusion of computer-mediated communication is so rapid that it makes rigorous and reliable research difficult. In spite of the close expiration dates, new research and fresh approaches are needed if we are to inspire students to make the best use of electronic collaboration tools.

Many high-tech Internet-related possibilities have the potential to make learning more interactive, exploratory, and inquiry based. However, the most important factor involved in exploiting that potential is quality teaching. Good teachers make for good schools and for the appropriate use of technology. Approaching the glut of increasingly complex information makes the guidance of well-trained teachers more important than ever. When teachers know how to tap into student knowledge and comfort with technology, Internet resources can help with academic achievement by opening doors to the world in which students are growing up. This process can help to link learning to real-life experiences so that students can retain and apply new information in meaningful ways.

The boundaries between the schools and the outside world are becoming more and more permeable. In the new knowledge society, institutions and individuals outside the school are increasingly playing a role in engaging students. Technologists need to recognize this reality and keep an eye on the bigger picture so that they avoid the tunnel vision that can lead promising technologies down blind alleys. As plans for integrating technology into the curriculum move ahead, schools and districts will need to establish proficiency standards and long-term plans for technology-related professional development. At the same time, schools of education will have to do a better job of preparing new teachers to use digital media and Internet resources.

Those involved directly with the schools need to explore how technologies may change the way we teach and learn. Students and teachers need to know how to use the latest information and communication for more than duplicating traditional practices. Teachers need more than a knowledge of their subject and an understanding of the characteristics of effective instruction. They must also know how to use the most powerful media of their times to teach subject matter effectively. Far from replacing teachers, the latest technology makes skillful teachers more important than ever. Many institutions and individuals may have a role to play, but nothing can replace a good teacher and collaborative peer interaction in the classroom.

References

Angeles, Rebecca. The authors acknowledge her major contributions to this chapter.

Brown, N. (1999). *Young children's literacy development and the role of televisual texts.* New York: Falmer Press.

Burbules, N. C. (2000). *Watch IT: The risks and promises of information technologies for education.* Boulder, CO: WestView Press.

Calvert, S. L. (1999). *Children's journey through the information age.* Princeton, NJ: McGraw-Hill.

De Cicco, E., Farmer, M., & Hargrave, C. (1999). *Activities for using the Internet in primary schools.* Dover, New Hampshire: Kogan Page.

DiSessa, A. A. (2000). *Changing minds: Computers, learning, and literacy.* Cambridge, MA: MIT Press.

Goldman-Segall, R. (1998). *Points of viewing children's thinking: A digital ethnographer's journey.* Mahwah, NJ: Erlbaum.

Gordon, D. T. (2000). *The digital classroom: How technology is changing the way we teach and learn.* Cambridge, MA: Harvard Education Letter.

Hanna, D. E., Glowacki-Dudka, M., & Conceicao-Runlee, S. (2000). *147 practical tips for teaching online groups: Essentials of Web-based education.* Madison, WI: Atwood.

Hawke, C. S. (2000). *Computer and Internet use on campus: A legal guide to issues of intellectual property, free speech, and privacy,* Somerset, NJ: Wiley.

Hoffman, D. D. (1998). *Visual intelligence: How we create what we see.* Scranton, PA: Norton.

International Technology Education Association. (2000). *Standards for technological literacy: Content for the study of technology.* Englewood, CO: Author.

Jasmine, G. & Cain, J, (2000). *Early childhood activities with Internet connections.*

Jones, G., Toffler, A., & Toffler, H. (2000). *Cyberschools : An education renaissance,* Englewood, CO: Jones Interactive.

Junion-Metz, G. (2000). *Coaching Kids for the Internet: A Guide for librarians, teachers, and parents* (Internet Workshop Series No. 9). Berkeley, CA: Library Solutions Press.

Linn, M. C. (1999). *Computers, teachers, peers: Science learning partners.* Mahwah, NJ: Erlbaum.

Mandel family. (1999). *Cyberspace for kids : 600 Sites that are kid-tested & parent approved* (Grades 1–2). Grand Rapids, MI: Authors.

Mandel family, Jackson, P., and Bucella, M. (1999). *Cyberspace for kids* (Grades 3–4). Grand Rapids, MI: Authors.

Rosenberg, M. J. (2000). *E-learning: Strategies for delivering knowledge in the digital age.* Princeton, NJ: McGraw-Hill.

Salmon, G. (2000). *E-moderating: The key to teaching and learning online.* Sterling, VA: Stylus.

Salvador, R. (2000). *The best-ever Web sites for the topics you teach.* New York: Scholastic.

Schweizer, H. (1999). *Designing and teaching an on-line course:*

Spinning your Web classroom. Needham Heights, MA: Allyn & Bacon.

Spitzer, M. (1999). *The mind within the net: Models of learning, thinking, and acting.* Cambridge, MA: MIT Press.

Stoll, C. (1999). *High tech heretic: Why computers don't belong in the classroom and other reflections by a computer contrarian.* New York: Doubleday.

Story-Huffman, R. (1999). *Caldecott on the Net: Reading & Internet.* Fort Atkinson, WI: Highsmith Press.

Appendix: Suggested Resources for Teaching and Learning on the Web

There are many good Internet Web sites for teachers and students. Online resources include access to discussion groups, virtual classrooms, research tools, free software, and many other tools to help teachers and students integrate the Internet into their daily work. We have chosen a sampling of sites that work across a number of subjects and grade levels.

Evaluating Information on the Internet

- Esther Grassian, "Thinking Critically about World Wide Web Resources," UCLA College Library Instruction http://www.library.ucla.edu/libraries/college/instruct/web/critical.htm
- Elizabeth E. Kirk, "Evaluating Information Found on the Internet" http://milton.mse.jhu.edu:8001/research/education/net.html#b)
- Internet Detective http://sosig.ac.uk/desire/internet-detective.html)
- Pamela Mendels, "Study Shows Students Use Internet Primarily for Research," *The New York Times*, April 28, 1998, Web site, http://www.nytimes.com.
- Jan Alexander and Marsha Ann Tate, *Web wisdom: How to Evaluate and Create Information Quality on the Web*. Mahwah, NJ: Lawrence Erlbaum Associates, 1999.

Educational Resources

- Educational Resources Information Center (ERIC): http://www.accesseric.org/
- Teachers@Work: http://www.teachers-work.com
- Discovery School: http://www.discoveryschool.com
- Learn2.com: http://www.learn2.com
- Houghton Mifflin Education Place: http://www.Eduplace.com
- Classroom Connect: http://www.ClassroomConnect.com

- Microsoft in Education: http://www.Microsoft.com/education/k12
- Federal Resources for Education: http://www.ed.gov/free
- The Web Teacher: http://www.webteacher.com
- Educyberstor.com: http://www.teachingk-12.com
- StarChild: http://starchild.gsfc.nasa.gov/docs/StarChild/StarChild.html
- The Teel Home Education Page: http://teelfamily.com/education
- The Smithsonian: http://www.si.edu/newstart.htm
- History/Social Studies Web Site for K–12 Teachers: http://www.execpc.com/~dboals/boals.htm
- Web Quest: http://edweb.sdsu.edu/webquest/webquest.html
- California Technology Assistance Project: http://www.ctap.k12.ca.us
- Classroom of the Future Foundation: http://www. sdcoe.k12.ca.us/jrrtc/lotf.htm
- Allen Communication: http://www.allencomm.com
- Tapped-in: http://www.tappedin.org
- Knowledge Integration Environment Project: http://www.kie.berkeley.edu/KIE.html
- The Computer Museum: http://www.mos.org/tcm/tcm.html
- Delphion Intellectual Property Network (replace IBM Patent Server: http://www.delphion.com/
- Mars Pathfinder Mission: http://mars.jpl.nasa.gov/default.html
- Exploratorium: ExploraNet: http://www.exploratorium .edu
- "Paleontology Without Walls": http://www .ucmp.berkeley.edu/exhibit/exhibits.html
- WIRED Magazine: http://www.wired.com
- CNET Technology News: http://www.cnet.com
- Techtv Channel: http://www.techtv.com
- Yahooligans: The Web Guide for Kids: http://www.yahooligans.com

Constructing and Designing Web Pages

You may find more detailed instructions and the latest techniques on Web page design and construction from the following sources:

- Web Pages for Absolute Beginners: http://subnet.virtual-pc.com/li542871/index.html
- Web Monkey for Kids: http://hotwired.lycos.com/webmonkey/kids/
- Microsoft FrontPage in the Classroom: http://www.actden.com/fp/
- Home Page Central: http://home.learn2.com/
- AT&T WorldNet Service: http://home.att.net/
- Community Network: Creating Web Pages (Introductory Level): http://www.cln.org/themes/webpages_intro.html
- SofWeb: Using the Internet: http://www.sofweb.vic.edu.au/internet/publish.htm
- Learn2.com: http://www.learn2.com/
- AT&T WorldNet Service: http://home.att.ne

Glossary

artificial intelligence (AI) — computer programs that try to emulate the decision-making capabilities of the human mind; the field of research that attempts to emulate human intelligence in a machine. Fields within AI include knowledge-based systems, expert systems, pattern recognition, automatic learning, natural-language understanding, and robotics. The promise of artificial intelligence keeps receding as we reach out to capture some of our sci-fiction fantasies.

assimilation — to take in; to incorporate new knowledge.

auto focus — a camera that focuses automatically.

bilingual/bicultural — the processing of two or more languages and/or cultures.

Bioinformatics — a field of study combining genetics and molecular biology.

bit — a contraction of the phrase "binary digit." In binary code, one of the two possible values, usually zero and one.

book club — a small-group, student-led discussion of topics and issues related to a text.

boolean search — powerful tools for conducting sophisticated computer searches.

bots — individualized search engines for specific information.

broadband technology — high-speed Internet service, cable service, and local and long distance phone service over cable. With broadband technology, the classroom can provide students with a vast amount of resources. Information gathering is much faster, Internet access is always available, and visual support in the classroom is readily available.

browser — an instrument that implements access to information spaces, and helps to put the user in touch with information: for example, the Web browser NESTOR runs on Microsoft Windows.

buttons — a way of inserting links in the program, on which the viewer can click to move from one display to another. The buttons may be contained in key words highlighted in the text or in graphic symbols.

byte — a contraction for "by eight." A group of bits clustered together to store one unit of information on a computer. A byte may correspond, for example, to a letter of the English alphabet.

chip — a collection of related circuits that work together on a task or set of tasks, residing on a wafer of semiconductor material (typically silicon).

classification strategies — instructional activities that enable the learner to access, elaborate, and integrate concepts by placing them within a systematic organizational structure.

classifying — grouping things by properties or functions.

collaborative group — a group of students with varying abilities working together to solve a problem or complete a learning task.

comprehension — understanding.

computation — the process of calculating a result by use of an algorithm; the ability to remember and solve problems.

constancy — the ways in which systems do not change.

constructivism — a child-centered view of learning that holds that each child constructs a knowledge of science by him or herself.

constructivist model of reading — a model in which the reader draws on text information and prior knowledge to construct text meaning during reading.

continuous partial attention — this term refers to people being distracted by multiple sources of information. They listen to the radio, work the Internet, have the TV set going in the background, and try to carry on a conversation at the same time.

controlling variables — a science process controlling the conditions that cause an event to occur.

cooperative learning — an arrangement in which students work in mixed-ability groups and are rewarded on the basis of the success of the group.

culturally biased — the term used for assessment tests that usually yield significantly lower scores for racial, ethnic, and socioeconomic minorities.

culturally diverse students — a reference to "minority" students.

cut away — to trim a piece of film.

cut in — the act of copying text from one location in a document, deleting it, and then inserting it in another location.

cybernetics — a term coined by Norbert Wiener to describe the "science of control and communication in animals and machines." Cybernetics is based on the theory that intelligent living things adapt to their environments and accomplish objectives primarily by reacting to feedback from their surroundings.

cyberspace — a "consensual hallucination"; the Internet is often a vehicle that puts students in touch with each other in a technologically-enabled network that supports human communication and information exchange.

database — the structured collection of data that is designed in connection with an information retrieval system. A database management system allows monitoring, updating, and interacting with the database.

debugging — the process of discovering and correcting errors in computer hardware and software. The issue of bugs or errors in a program will become increasingly important as computers are integrated into the human brain and physiology throughout the 21st century.

density — ratio of the mass of an object to its volume.

desktop publishing — a collaborative task of multiple authors creating a coproduced document that may contain the various features of multimedia.

digital — varying in discrete steps. The use of combinations of bits to represent data in computation; contrasted with analog.

digital equipment — equipment using computer calculations.

digitisation — transferred to a computer storage medium by first coding as numbers.

discourse — conversation, written or oral treatment of a particular subject.

dissolves — to fade gradually into another shot.

diversity — a variety of choices in which evolution thrives.

downloading — to bring information to a computer from a network or from a computer to a disk.

e-books — books that are read on handheld computers called *Readers*. Electronic readers can download books, magazines, and journals from the Internet. Many have features such as a color touch screen that allows the user to access verbal explanations and related topics. It is possible to adjust the size of the print, the sound, and the background lighting. Some of the newer electronic books even allow viewing of related video clips. All of these handheld (book-size) devices can easily load up a number of titles and supporting material. Nonfiction works can be constantly upgraded, and books can be customized so that the user can read only certain parts.

e-mail — electronic mail; messages or notes sent via telecommunications; can be accessed by sending a message from one person to one or more other people.

file system — the product created by a database program; any collection of data stored on a computer medium.

fill lights — lights that soften a scene and often pick up details.

flashbacks — an interruption in the continuity of a story.

foreground — the part of the scene nearest the viewer.

frame — to form or construct according to a pattern or design.

framing — the balance or symmetry in a frame.

globalization — a policy outlook that is worldwide in scope.

graphics — a form of visual artistic representation, such as painting, drawing, or etching.

hard lighting — lighting that creates clearly defined shadows.

heterogeneous — differing in structure; dissimilar.

"hits" on the Web — a way of knowing that others are connecting to your data.

hollywood editing — a traditional editing style consisting of medium shot, long shot, and close-up shot.

hypermedia — combines text, sound, animation, and graphics to create teaching aids, reports, or projects. The use of Hypermedia inevitably puts students in charge of developing a project and constructing both knowledge and problem-solving strategies.

hypertext — Text in electronic form that has been indexed and linked (hyperlinks) by software in a variety of ways so that users can randomly and interactively conduct "searches" on the Internet.

icon — a picture or symbol used to present a concept or an idea.

independent variable — a variable that is changed or manipulated.

inferring — a science process drawing an inference from data; to interpret or explain observations.

inquiry — the process of finding answers through problem solving; posing questions, a habit of mind. Inquiry cannot exist without curiosity.

integrated language arts — an approach to literacy instruction that links reading, writing, listening, and language skills.

interdisciplinary literacy instruction — integration of content-area learning with literacy.

Internet and **World Wide Web** — a system that enables us to communicate instantly across national and international borders and that has the potential to change the ways that students interact with texts, making them more active participants in their reading.

investigating — a science process that involves finding out about the physical world.

jigsaw editing — arranging short video segments to design a coherent film or video.

logo — a high-level programming language originally designed as an AI language but later popularized by Seymour Papert as an environment to allow children to learn problem-solving behaviors and skills.

Mosaic — one of the first programs designed to allow Internet resources to be displayed graphically rather than just in text.

mouse — input device that a computer user moves around on the table beside the computer in order to control a pointer on a screen and presses down (clicks) in order to select options from the screen.

multimedia — a computer system that incorporates text, sound, pictures and graphics and/or video; a seamless integration of two or more media (text, sound, graphics, motion).

MUDs/MOOS (Multi User Domains) — a simulated environment in which users type in descriptions of "rooms" that others may visit on-line.

nanotechnology — a technology that was suggested more than 40 years ago by Nobel Prize winner Richard Feynman, who said that scientists could make materials by manipulating matter at the atomic level to build tiny machines that could construct even smaller machines (as small as molecules). Now nanotechnology has started to move from wishful thinking to reality. Researchers have even integrated nanoscale technologies into living systems. "Nanomechanics" have engineered bionic motors that can be fused to genetically engineered molecules and used in everything from data storage to graphical display technologies.

network — a series of computers connected through cabeling or wireless methods to share programs through a central file server computer.

neural network — a type of AI program designed to work like a human brain and nervous system.

node — one station or site on a computer network.

observing — science process according to which the senses are used to gain information about the natural world.

online — being connected to a computer system in operation.

pacing — human interaction or range of emotions.

pans — panoramic shots.

PBS — public broadcasting station.

peer tutoring — individual or small-group tutoring by students of the same age.

portfolio — a container of documents that show proficiency or mastery of subject material.

preconception — to form an opinion beforehand.

procedural knowledge — knowledge that can be actualized.

process skills — the word *process* is often used to describe active learning, "doing" rather than "knowing that"; processes are a series of actions. The term *science process skills* originated in the 1960s. Although the processes have remained about the same, the terminology has changed. Today math and science educators talk about *active learning processes*. Process skills include observing, questioning, classifying, ordering, communicating, measuring, predicting, inferring, investigating, and experimenting.

predicting — a science process that involves foretelling future occurrences.

production — manipulation of technology tools.

reciprocal teaching — a social process in which explanations are exchanged, learning from a knowledgeable authority.

reflective understanding — the teacher's knowledge of students' perceptions of their own learning, usually obtained through class-room observation or questioning students about what they think, feel, or are doing during a learning task.

rhythm — a series of steps that form successive stages.

scaffolding — layers of meaning conveyed through photos or drawings; a strategy in which teachers provide students with modeling and support to help them acquire a skill.

scientific concepts — abstract, systematized knowledge, usu-ally learned by children during formal schooling.

search engines — programs designed to help users find infor-mation on the Web pages of the Internet; this could be informa-tion on sound, video, graphics, and text files.

sequencing — part of the ordering system, putting things in order.

simulation — a type of software that models a real or imaginary system in order to reach the principles on which the system is based; the representation of the behavior or characteristics of one system through the use of another system.

soft lighting — creates a diffused illumination.

sound bridges — sound transitions from scene to scene.

spider — a special kind of software that searches the Web to find new text, organize it, and index it.

splice — to join by weaving together the end strands.

spreadsheet — software designed to store data (usually, but not always, numeric) by row-column positions known as cells; can also be used to do calculations on the data.

storyboard — a visual sketch of how scenes will happen in a production.

streaming audio — a state-of-the-art live voice innovative technology that can be included on a Web site to create a powerful message that jumps off the Web page.

streaming video — motion video with accompanying audio delivered "live" over the Internet; users do not have to download a file to their computers in order to activate and play it.

syntax — the structure of language or rules that govern how words work together in phrases, clauses, and sentences.

system — an organized collection of objects or concepts that have some influence on one another, constituting a whole.

technology — an evolving process of tool creation to shape and control the environment. Technology goes beyond the mere fashioning and use of tools. It involves a record of tool making and a progression in the sophistication of tools. It requires invention and is itself a continuation by other means.

telecommunications — communications over a distance made possible by a computer and modem or a distance learning system such as broadcast TV.

theme — the integration of concepts with facts to link structures of various disciplines.

tilt — to cause to slope or tip.

tutorial — type of instructional software that offers a complete sequence of instruction on a given topic.

underlight — part of a lighting setup creating a mood: lighting from below. This usually adds depth to a scene.

V.A.I. (Video as Input) — a new immersion technology that is appearing in computer games and activities with names like VBall (an on-screen volleyball game) and Horse (a basketball shooting contest), these games represent richer "virtual reality" action that can be controlled without a keyboard or any other physical input device. The games work by making both the game and the player virtual. Some speculate that the technology could have applications for students in virtual classrooms or to interact with others around the world at a computer-generated conference.

videodisc — a storage medium designed for storing pictures, short video sequences, and movies.

virtual reality — technically used to describe human-computer interfaces that enable users to experience physical sensations through sight, hearing, and touch, giving a feeling of actual presence and movement in a place where there is none. These images allow one to participate in a virtual game, fly a plane, or manipulate surgical instruments in a delicate operation.

virus — a program written with the purpose of doing harm or mischief to programs, data, and/or hardware components of a computer system.

voice recognition — the capability provided by a computer and program to respond predictably to speech commands.

VRML Chat Systems — (virtual reality) interactive representations of physical reality.

window — a box in a graphic user interface that appears when one opens a disk or folder to display its contents.

word processing — an applications software activity that uses the computer for typing and preparing documents.

World Wide Web — A highly distributed network allowing individuals and organizations around the world to communicate with one another. Communications include the sharing of text, images, sounds, video, and software.

WWW plug-ins — an item that allows Netscape Navigator to view and manipulate a variety of files that it was not originally designed to handle. Using the right plug-in, one can view Word documents, Excel spreadsheets, Quick Time videos, and other files that have been embedded in Web pages.

Index

activities
    for cooperative problem solving, 2, 35
    for discussing technology, 60–62
    vital technologies activities, 60–62
advertising, 10, 11, 130–133
    in lesson planning, 130, 131
camcorder tips, 42–46
collaboration and change, 81, 82
    a shared journey into a new century, 85, 86
    activities, 73–81
collaborative,
    digital tools, 65
    learning techniques, 64
    possibilities for collaboration, 57, 58, 65–70
communication,
    changes, 7, 8, 11, 12
    process, 7, 8, 95–97
comparing, 94
composer, 170
    adding graphic files, 174, 175
    adding hyperlinks, 173
constructing meaning, 132
constructivist learning, 34
    and media tools, 34, 35
create a simple web site, 169–178
    adding graphics, 174, 175
    adding hyperlinks, 173
    inserting sound, 175, 176
curriculum,
    and teachers, 22, 25
    and technology-mediated literacies, 124–126, 129
digital technology, 2, 3, 20
    and student motivation, 8, 9, 21, 22
    possibilities of, 30
discovering processes, 91–94
e-books, 15–18
editing, video, 44–46
education goals and technology, 21, 22

estimating, 99
experimenting, 99, 100
    approaches to, 30
    judgments, 30
    process of, 30, 31
forming relationships, 94
future of technological possibilities, 17, 18
graphing, 96
group study, 66, 67
guidelines for evaluating information on the Internet, 149–154
    questions, 152–154
inferring, 93
Internet, the, 6, 7, 145–179
    and interactive learning, 24–26
    guidelines for teaching, 27–30
    history of, 145
    positives of the Internet, 146–148
    practical classroom possibilities, 146–148, 162–178
    safety on the Internet, 6, 154–157
    survey result of educators and students, 148
literacy, technological, 1–5, 33, 62–65, 123–143
    at home and school, 13–15
    role models and change, 133–136
meaningful learning and media education, 33, 34
measuring, 93
media,
    characteristics, of, 7
    and children, 7, 8, 11, 12, 19, 20
    and consumers, 23, 24
    and literacy, 3, 33, 36, 50
media literacy, 3
    definition of, 33
    goals of, 50
    old and new literacies, 36
media scavenger hunt, 137

National Science Education Standards, 126, 127
observing, 92
off-line activities, 134, 162–166
parents' and teachers' roles in explaining media messages, 131–133
practical Internet classroom activities, 233–247
predicting, 98, 99
process skills, 89–119
    activities, 100–112
    and questioning 90
    key process skills, 91
problem solving, 1, 69–71
    group model for, 70, 71
production techniques, 41
    ideas for student production, 46–48
reciprocal teaching 82, 83
reviewing the process skills, 112, 113
safety on the Internet, 6, 154–157
sample
    off-line activities, 134, 162–166
    thematic activities, 116–119
sequencing, 94
sharing, 97
social skills, 56, 57
standards,
    and language arts, 128, 129
    and technological design, 127
    and theatre, 128, 129
    technology and science, 126, 127
storyboards, 38–40
    creating a storyboard, 38, 39
    definition of, 38
    storyboard techniques, 40
teachers,
    and media production, 48–51
    and media goals, 50
teaching, learning, and literacy, 50
team work, 67
    and group roles, 69
technological literacy, 1–5, 33, 62–65, 123–143
    and popular culture, 123, 124

sample off-line activities, 134, 162–166
technology,
    impact of, 7, 20, 21
    and teachers, 6, 7, 10, 14, 25, 26, 48, 142
    lessons from yesteryear, 58, 59
    shaping the use of technology in the schools, 6, 10, 25, 33, 178, 179
    tools, 34, 35
television,
    and children, 12, 19, 20
    and media, 123–125, 131–133
    lessons of, 10, 11
thematic units, 113–117
    developing, 114–117
valuing, 95
video,
    and society, 37
    history of, 36, 37
    production, 35, 36, 41–48
        adding sound and graphics, 6, 157–159
        and problem solving, 36, 37
        and student attitude, 35
visual,
    imagery, 22
    technologies for the 20th century, 58–62
        activity, 60–62
    using,
        data, 96
        language, 97
Web cam, 146
    basic principles, 157–159
    creating classroom material, 157
    hardware and software, 159–161
Web sites, 146
    suggested, 146, 147
World wide web,
    create a simple web site, 169–178
    adding graphics, 174, 175
    adding hyperlinks, 173
    inserting sound, 175, 176
    report card, 146

The Authors

Dennis Adams is a professor of education who teaches in the public schools when the university is not in session. He is a former Fulbright Scholar who had done graduate work at the University of California and Harvard University. After receiving a PhD in Curriculum and Instruction from the University of Wisconsin he has written more than a dozen books and over a hundred articles. His research and writing projects have focused on topics such as language learning, technological innovation, teacher education, collaborative inquiry, and literacy for diverse populations.

Mary Hamm is a professor at San Francisco State University. She was a public school teacher in Wisconsin before receiving a MA degree in Environmental Education from the University of Wisconsin. Her doctorate is from the University of Northern Colorado. She has authored more than ten books and has published articles in journals such as *Science and Children*, *School Science and Mathematics*, and *Educational Technology*.